The Word of God

Its Nature and Content

Other Books by Dr. Arnold G. Fruchtenbaum

Jesus Was a Jew

A Passover Haggadah for Jewish Believers

The Remnant of Israel:
The History, Theology, and Philosophy of the Messianic Jewish Community

Ha-Mashiach: The Messiah of the Hebrew Scriptures

The Footsteps of the Messiah:
A Study of the Sequence of Prophetic Events

Israelology: The Missing Link in Systematic Theology

An Historical and Geographical Study Guide of Israel:
With a Supplement on Jordan

The Sabbath

God's Will & Man's Will:
Predestination, Election, and Free Will

Ariel's Bible Commentary Series:

The Messianic Jewish Epistles

Judges and Ruth

The Book of Genesis

Biblical Lovemaking: A Study of the Song of Solomon

The Word of God

Its Nature and Content

Arnold G. Fruchtenbaum
Th.M., Ph.D.

© 2014 by Ariel Ministries
2nd Edition, © 2015 by Ariel Ministries

ISBN 978-1-935174-47-9

Library of Congress Control Number:
2014954514

REL101000 RELIGION / Messianic Judaism

All rights reserved. No part of this publication may be reproduced, distributed, or transmitted in any form or by any means, including photocopying, recording, or other electronic or mechanical methods, without the prior written permission of the publisher, except in the case of brief quotations embodied in critical reviews and certain other noncommercial uses permitted by copyright law. For permission requests, write to the publisher at the address below.

All Scripture quotations, unless otherwise noted, are from the *1901 American Standard Version* (Oak Harbor, WA: Logos Research Systems, Inc., 1994). However, the archaic language has been changed with one exception: The archaic *ye* has been retained in order to distinguish the second person plural from the singular *you*. The words *Jesus* and *Christ* have been replaced with *Yeshua* and *Messiah*.

Editor: Christiane Jurik
Contributing Editor: Chris Eisbrenner
Proofreaders: Pauline Ilsen, Joni Bohannon
Printed in the United States of America
Cover illustration by Jesse and Josh Gonzales (*http://www.vipgraphics.net*)

Published by Ariel Ministries
P.O. Box 792507
San Antonio, TX 78279-2507
www.ariel.org

This volume is dedicated to

Bill and Debbie Byars

whose love for the Word and its Jewish background has brought them to Ariel Ministries and who have continued to be helpful to the ministry to this day.

Contents

CHAPTER I
INTRODUCTION 1

CHAPTER II
THE NATURE OF THE BIBLE 5

  A. The Key Terms 5
  B. Attitudes toward the Bible 6
      1. Rationalism 7
      2. Mysticism 7
      3. Romanism 8
      4. Neo-Orthodoxy 9
      5. Cults 9
      6. Orthodoxy 10
  C. The Wonders of the Bible 11
      1. Formation 11
      2. Preservation 11
      3. Subject Matter 13
      4. Influence 14
  D. The Supernatural Origin of the Bible 14
      1. The Book of God 14
      2. The Problem of Sin 15
      3. Ethics and Morals 15
      4. Continuity 16
      5. Prophecies 16
      6. Types and Antitypes 16
      7. Literary Value 17
      8. Absence of Prejudice 17
      9. Scientific Accuracy 17
      10. Enduring Freshness 18
  E. Questions and Study Suggestions 19

CHAPTER III
THE BIBLE AND DIVINE REVELATION 21

   A. General Revelation 22
      1. The Nature of General Revelation 22
      2. The Means of General Revelation 22
      3. The Limitations of General Revelation 24
   B. Special Revelation 26
      1. The Nature of Special Revelation 26
      2. The Necessity of Special Revelation 26
      3. The Means of Special Revelation 27
         a. Theophanies 28
         b. Miracles 28
           (1) The Definition of Miracles 28
           (2) The Nature of Miracles 29
           (3) Two Types of Miracles 29
           (4) The Facets of Miracles 30
           (5) The Frequency of Miracles 30
           (6) The Vocabulary of Miracles 30
           (7) The Purpose of Miracles 31
         c. Direct Communication 31
         d. Angels 34
         e. Incarnation 34
         f. Scriptures 34
   C. Progressive Revelation 36
   D. Questions and Study Suggestions 37

CHAPTER IV
THE INSPIRATION OF THE SCRIPTURES 39

   A. Definition 39
      1. God's Superintendence 39
      2. Human Authors 40
      3. Inerrancy 40
      4. God's Revelation 41
   B. Theories of Inspiration 41
      1. Key Issue: Dual Authorship 41

2. False Theories 43
    a. Natural or Intuition Theory 43
    b. Mystical or Illumination Theory 43
    c. Partial Inspiration Theory 44
    d. Degrees Inspiration Theory 44
    e. Conceptual Inspiration Theory 44
    f. Dynamic Inspiration Theory 45
    g. Mechanical or Dictation Inspiration Theory 45
    h. Neo-Orthodox Theory 46
3. The True Position: Plenary Verbal Inspiration 46
    a. The Position 46
        (1) Five Things Plenary Verbal Inspiration Did not Accomplish 47
        (2) Five Things Plenary Verbal Inspiration Did Accomplish 48
    b. Evidence for Plenary Verbal Inspiration 49
        (1) Key Passages 49
        (2) Other Lines of Evidence 51
    d. Objections to Plenary Verbal Inspiration 55
        (1) Science and History 55
        (2) Skepticism of Prophecy and Miracles 56
        (3) Morals and Religions 56
        (4) New Testament Quotations of the Old Testament 57
    e. Conclusion 66
C. QUESTIONS AND STUDY SUGGESTIONS 67

CHAPTER V
THE COVENANTS OF THE BIBLE 69

A. THE TYPES OF COVENANTS 69
B. THE COVENANTS WITH ISRAEL 70
C. THE EDENIC COVENANT 71
  1. The Participants in the Covenant 71
  2. The Provisions of the Covenant 71
  3. Basis for a Dispensation and Present Status 73
D. THE ADAMIC COVENANT 74
  1. The Participants in the Covenant 74
  2. The Provisions of the Covenant 75
    a. The Serpent: Genesis 3:14 75
    b. Satan: Genesis 3:15 75

- c. The Woman: Genesis 3:16 76
- d. The Man: Genesis 3:17-19 76
- 3. Basis for a Dispensation and Present Status 77
- E. THE NOAHIC COVENANT 78
  - 1. The Participants in the Covenant 78
  - 2. The Provisions of the Covenant 78
  - 3. Basis for a Dispensation and Present Status: 80
- F. THE ABRAHAMIC COVENANT 81
  - 1. The Participants in the Covenant 82
  - 2. The Provisions of the Covenant 82
    - a. Abraham 83
    - b. Israel 83
    - c. Gentiles 84
  - 3. The Basis for Development of Other Covenants 84
  - 4. The Confirmation of the Covenant 84
  - 5. Basis for a Dispensation and Present Status 85
- G. THE MOSAIC COVENANT 86
  - 1. The Participants in the Covenant 86
  - 2. The Provisions of the Covenant 86
    - a. The Totality of the Law 87
    - b. The Blessings and Judgments of the Law 87
    - c. The Blood Sacrifice Added 87
    - d. The Diet Restrictions Imposed 87
    - e. The Death Penalty Expanded 88
    - f. The Sign of the Covenant 88
    - g. The Token of the Covenant 88
  - 3. Relationship to Previous Covenants 90
  - 4. The Purposes of the Law 90
    - a. To Reveal the Holiness of God 91
    - b. To Provide a Rule of Conduct 91
    - c. To Provide for Corporate Worship 91
    - d. To Keep Jews a Distinct People 91
    - e. To Serve as a Middle Wall of Partition 91
    - f. To Reveal Sin 92
    - g. To Make One Sin More 92
    - h. To Show Man's Inability to Please God 93
    - i. To Drive One to Faith 93
    - j. Summary 93

  5. The Present Status 93
    a. The Unity of the Law of Moses 94
    b. The Law of Moses Has Been Rendered Inoperative 95
    c. The Moral Law 98
    d. Matthew 5:17-18 98
    e. The Law of Messiah 99
    f. The Principle of Freedom 100
    g. The Sabbath 100
 H. THE LAND COVENANT 101
  1. The Participants in the Covenant 101
  2. The Provisions of the Covenant 101
  3. The Importance of the Covenant 103
  4. The Confirmation of the Covenant: Ezekiel 16:1-63 103
  5. The Present Status 104
 I. THE DAVIDIC COVENANT 104
  1. The Participants in the Covenant 104
  2. The Provisions of the Covenant 104
  3. The Importance of the Covenant 106
  4. The Confirmation of the Covenant 107
  5. Present Status 107
 J. THE NEW COVENANT 107
  1. The Participants in the Covenant 107
  2. The Provisions of the Covenant 108
  3. The Importance of the Covenant 111
  4. The Relationship of the Church to the New Covenant 111
  5. The Gentile Obligation 114
  6. Basis for a Dispensation and Present Status 114
 K. CONCLUSION 115
 L. QUESTIONS AND STUDY SUGGESTIONS 116

CHAPTER VI
THE DISPENSATIONS OF GOD 119

 A. DEFINITION 119
  1. Etymology 119
  2. Scripture Usage of the Words 120
  3. Definition 122
  4. The Facets of a Dispensation 124

- 5. The Mark of a Dispensationalist 124
  - a. What it is not 124
  - b. What it is 125
  - c. Conclusion 126
- B. THE DISPENSATIONS 126
  - 1. The Dispensation of Innocence or Freedom: Genesis 1:28-3:8 126
    - a. The Names 126
    - b. The Chief Person 127
    - c. Man's Responsibility 127
    - d. Man's Specific Test 127
    - e. Man's Failure 128
    - f. Man's Judgment 128
    - g. God's Display of Grace 128
  - 2. The Dispensation of Conscience or Self-Determination: Genesis 3:9-8:14 129
    - a. The Names 129
    - b. The Chief Person 129
    - c. Man's Responsibility 129
    - d. Man's Specific Test 130
    - e. Man's Failure 130
    - f. Man's Judgment 130
    - g. God's Display of Grace 131
  - 3. The Dispensation of Civil Government: Genesis 8:15-11:32 131
    - a. The Names 131
    - b. The Chief Person 131
    - c. Man's Responsibility 131
    - d. Man's Specific Test 132
    - e. Man's Failure 132
    - f. Man's Judgment 132
    - g. God's Display of Grace 133
  - 4. The Dispensation of Promise or Patriarchal Rule: Genesis 12:1 to Exodus 18:27 134
    - a. The Names 134
    - b. The Chief Person 134
    - c. Man's Responsibility 134
    - d. Man's Specific Test 134
    - e. Man's Failure 134

- f. Man's Judgment 135
- g. God's Display of Grace 135

5. The Dispensation of Law:
   Exodus 19:1 to Acts 1:26 135
   - a. The Name 135
   - b. The Chief Person 136
   - c. Man's Responsibility 136
   - d. Man's Specific Test 136
   - e. Man's Failure 136
   - f. Man's Judgment 137
   - g. God's Display of Grace 137

6. The Dispensation of Grace:
   Acts 2:1 to Revelation 19:21 138
   - a. The Name 138
   - b. The Chief Person 138
   - c. Man's Responsibility 138
   - d. Man's Specific Test 138
   - e. Man's Failure 139
   - f. Man's Judgment 139
   - g. God's Display of Grace 139

7. The Dispensation of the Kingdom or Millennium:
   Revelation 20:1-10 140
   - a. The Names 140
   - b. The Chief Person 140
   - c. Man's Responsibility 140
   - d. Man's Specific Test 140
   - e. Man's Failure 140
   - f. Man's Judgment 141
   - g. God's Display of Grace 141

8. Conclusion 141

C. QUESTIONS AND STUDY SUGGESTIONS 142

The Word of God

Chapter I
Introduction

What is Come and See?

Come and See is a multi-volume collection of messianic Bible studies transcribed from Dr. Arnold Fruchtenbaum's original radio broadcasts. Each study is a solid foundation upon which you can stand—a whiteboard from which you can teach— or a podium from which you can preach the uncompromised truth to your congregation. This extensive collection is replete with expert knowledge of Hebrew, Greek, the *Talmud*, the history of the Jews, the geography of *Eretz Yisrael*, the Land of Israel, a scholar's command of The Word—and the illumination of *Ruach HaKodesh* (the Holy Spirit). *Come and See* will edify you in your personal devotion or small group Bible study regardless of which topic you choose.

What Will You Discover in This Volume?

Volume 1 of *Come and See* is a collection of five messianic Bible studies pertaining to the Bible itself. This field of study is called *Bibliology*, the doctrine of the Scriptures. More specifically, the studies in this collection examine the revelation, inspiration, and divine program of the Bible. The first study deals with the nature of the Bible, the terms used for Scripture, its formation, authorship, linguistic make-up, influence in history, preservation, and subject matter. Differing "attitudes" or approaches to the Bible as found in rationalism, mysticism, Romanism, neo-orthodoxy, cults, and orthodoxy are also discussed. Study two deals with the concepts of God's "general revelation" to all humanity and His "specific revelation" through the Word of God, in all of its diverse modes. The third study examines the definition, proofs, and various theories of the inspiration of the Bible. In studies four and five, Dr. Fruchtenbaum discusses at length the covenants and dispensations of the Bible. Since much of God's relationship to man is based upon covenantal relationships, a study of the eight covenants is critical to understanding Scripture. A common way to divide the Bible is by dispensations, but dispensations are based on specific covenants, and knowledge of these covenants will help Bible readers to *rightly divide the word of truth* (II Tim. 2:15).

Questions and Study Suggestions for the Course

At the end of each chapter, you will find questions and study suggestions. The goal in implementing questions into this course is to bring application that is relevant to the subject. What is application, and what is the source of true application? Application of biblical truth is the working out of truth in life. This is manifested through behavior and words. The source of power for application is the Holy Spirit.

All too often after studying biblical truth, the question is asked: "How do I apply this truth to my life?" But if the source and power of applying truth to life is the Spirit of God, what is our true responsibility in application? Application can be viewed as the "green growth line" in one's life that is the result of diligently seeking truth. The "green growth line" is manifested obedience to truth through words and deeds. God's truth is the nurturing food of Scripture that the Holy Spirit uses to grow us in the image of Messiah.

What application is not is when a person believes he can make himself into the image of Messiah by reading truth and deciding on his own a plan of action that will bring spiritual growth.

The questions implemented in this course are questions to ponder in one's own heart and with fellow students and watch how the Spirit brings to our minds and our hearts those things that God wants us to know. Over time, we will acknowledge the work of the Spirit in our lives.

If one seeks truth, this course will give points of consideration that this author finds consistent with Holy Scripture. No matter what attitude is brought to this study, there will be interaction that creates thought provoking discussion. Intellectual integrity will be raised. When you complete this course, you may find a new power in life or you may find a stronger power in life. But no matter at what point of inquiry you begin this course of study, our prayer and desire is that you end the course with a new desire to know more about what is absolutely true and how truth can impact your life and the choices you make as you influence others.

Introduction

Get a Certificate of Completion!

In an effort to help reinforce your learning, we are also providing an exam for each volume of *Come and See*. As you complete each study, please visit us at www.ariel.org to take the Final Exam. Select *Come and See* from the menu options for details. The questions you will find online quiz your knowledge, while the questions at the end of each chapter are supposed to help you apply what you learned to your life. Upon successful completion of each exam, you will receive a Certificate of Completion.

Our desire is to provide a way for you to track through each study and monitor your progress. We would encourage you to study in small groups before taking the exams as a way to help prepare one another and stay accountable through each of the volumes.

The ultimate goal of this collection is for disciples of *Yeshua* (Jesus) to grow in their faith and to live out their calling to make disciples. We hope you enjoy the *Come and See Series*!

The Word of God

Chapter II
The Nature of the Bible

This chapter will look at the Scriptures to see what the Bible has to say about itself and to emphasize its uniqueness in four primary areas: the terms of the Bible; the attitudes toward the Bible; the wonders of the Bible; and the supernatural origin of the Bible.

A. The Key Terms

The first area is to delineate certain special terms or terminologies. There are four major terms concerning the holy writings to which believers adhere. The most common term is the word "Bible." This English word comes from the Greek word βίβλος (*biblos*), which means roll, book, or volume. Matthew 1:1 uses *biblos* to designate the "record" or "book" of the genealogy of *Yeshua* Messiah. βιβλίον (*biblion*), a diminutive of *biblos*, is used more frequently in Scripture and means "scroll" or "small book." Luke 4:17 uses *biblion* specifically to refer to the scroll of Isaiah the Prophet.

When the word "Bible" is mentioned today, we think of the Scriptures as a whole, combined in the form of a book, and the two Greek words can indeed mean the same. But it should be understood that more often they referred to only one segment, such as a specific book of the Bible. They were also used to refer to books in general, without a reference to anything sacred.

A second important term is the word "Scripture." The English term is a translation of the Greek word γραφὴ (*graphei*) which literally means "a writing" or "writings." In the Bible, the noun *graphei* is used 50 times in its various forms and always refers to the sacred and uniquely inspired books of the Bible. For example, in II Timothy 3:16, it is used of the Old Testament, calling it *God-breathed*. In II Peter 3:16, the very same word is also used of Paul's writings. This means that, in spite of Peter and Paul's dispute in Galatians 2, Peter fully recognized that the writings of Paul were Scripture. He called them *graphei*, a term used by the Jews to refer to the Old Testament.[1]

So the Greek word *graphei*, translated as "Scripture," means "writings." It was used of sacred books which were regarded as being part of God's inspired word to mankind.

A third term, "The Word of God," is a very common substitute for the terms Bible and Scripture in our day. This expression, ὁ λόγος τοῦ θεοῦ, is used in Scripture of both the Old and New Testaments to emphasize the revelation of God in written form. For example, in Matthew 15:6, the term "the Word of God" is used specifically in reference to the Law of Moses. In John 10:35, this term is used of the Old Testament as a whole, and in Hebrews 4:12 it is used of all Scripture referring to both the Old and New Testaments. Finally, in Romans 3:2, we find its plural form, τὰ λόγια τοῦ θεοῦ, translated as "the oracles of God."

The fourth main term is "Testament." The word "testament" is not nearly as common as the terms Bible, Scripture, or Word of God. It basically means "covenant." It is used to distinguish between the Old Covenant and the New Covenant, the Old Testament and the New Testament. The word is used particularly in dealing with the specific, unique covenants of Scripture.[2]

B. Attitudes toward the Bible

Over the course of history, people have adopted different attitudes toward the Bible. These attitudes can be divided into six basic categories: rationalism, mysticism, Romanism, neo-orthodoxy, cults, and orthodoxy.

---

[1] Question 1 on page 19

[2] Study Suggestion 1 on page 19

1. Rationalism

The main tenet of rationalism is that the mind is supreme. There are basically two forms of rationalism: extreme rationalism and moderate rationalism. Extreme rationalism denies the possibility of God's revealing Himself, especially through a written document such as the Scriptures. This is the view of atheism and agnosticism. In the earlier days of American history, extreme rationalism included the theology of deism, which was the theology of many of the American forefathers.

Moderate rationalism allows for the possibility of some revelation from God, but goes on saying that the human mind is the final judge of the validity of revelation. Today, moderate rationalism is exemplified by modernism and religious liberalism.[3]

2. Mysticism

The main doctrine of mysticism is that experience is supreme. In other words, if it fits our experience, it is correct and valid, but if it does not fit our experience, it is invalid. Those who hold this attitude claim that normative revelation cannot be received in a normal way. They will look at the Bible and agree that it is the Word of God, but they will go on to say that the Word of God is not complete; that there is more spiritual and divine truth available to souls that are "quickened" to receive it. They hold to added spiritual truths beyond the Scriptures. This type of false mysticism is exemplified by the theology of pantheism, Quakerism, and Thomas á Kempis

However, there is a form of true mysticism, which is the illumination of the mind by the Holy Spirit through the Scriptures. Biblical illumination (true mysticism) does not add truth to the Bible, nor is it an added experience by which one can judge or interpret the Bible. Rather, true mysticism is the illumination which we receive from the Holy Spirit in order to understand the Word of God. This is affirmed by Jude 3:

> *Beloved, while I was giving all diligence to write unto you of our common salvation, I was constrained to write unto you exhorting you to contend earnestly for the faith which was once for all delivered unto the saints.*

---

[3] Question 2 on page 19

Jude tells believers to "contend for the faith." The expression "the faith" (τῇ πίστει), using the definite article, refers to the whole body of truth that had already been delivered once for all to the church saints by the apostles, which is the written Word of God. Thus, true mysticism is affirmed by Jude 3 in that our understanding of the Scriptures must be in conformity with the Word of God as we rely on the faith delivered once and for all to the saints. We do not look for mystical experiences in order to try to learn truth beyond the Bible; instead we look for illumination by the Holy Spirit to properly understand it.

A true biblical mystic believes that the Bible is the final authority and that Scripture must judge all of his experiences; he must not permit his experience to become the judge of Scripture.[4]

3. Romanism

A third attitude towards the Scriptures is that of Romanism, or Roman Catholicism, which teaches that the church is supreme. Romanism teaches that the Bible is the product of the church, so the church can be its only interpreter. Romanism holds that the Scriptures are incomplete, and there is more truth available through the church. Romanism strongly emphasizes the obscurity of the Scriptures, claiming them hard to understand, and because they are obscure, only the church has the authority to properly clarify them.

Romanism gives a tremendous amount of authority to church tradition. It also tends to give priority of authority to the Latin Vulgate instead of the Hebrew and Greek Scriptures. Although it is only a translation from the original Hebrew and Greek, the Latin Vulgate is often given priority over the original Hebrew Old Testament and the Greek New Testament.

Furthermore, tied into this view of Scripture is the concept of apostolic succession. Romanists teach that Peter was the first Pope and that, by means of "apostolic succession," papal authority has been handed down from Pope to Pope throughout all generations. Because of this apostolic succession found only in the Roman church, only the Roman church has the truth of what the Bible actually means, and they must determine the meaning for believers. This is why they believe the church is supreme.[5]

---

[4] Question 3 on page 19

[5] Question 4 on page 19

4. Neo-Orthodoxy

Neo-orthodoxy teaches that the encounter is supreme. According to neo-orthodox theology, the Bible is a fallible witness to the revelation of God in the Word, which was the Messiah. In addition, they say that the Bible is not the Word of God, but it does contain the Word of God. It is for the individual to determine what the Word of God within the Bible is and what is not. To clearly understand what is and what is not the Word of God, there is the need for some type of divine encounter. Even though they all emphasize the need of a divine encounter, none of them agree with each other exactly what this divine encounter is about and how one knows whether or not he has had one!

Furthermore, they disagree among themselves on what is the Word of God within the Bible and what is not. Because they do not believe that the Bible is the Word of God, but that it only contains the Word of God, they become the final judge themselves as to what in the Bible is considered the Word of God and what is not. Because the encounter is supreme, everyone can have his own encounter and still come up with totally different conclusions.[6]

5. Cults

Basically, the cults teach that the Bible plus the writing of someone else are of equal, if not greater authority. This is the key mark of a cult. For instance, Mormonism has *The Book of Mormon* that they consider to be inspired. Christian Science has Mary Baker Eddy's book, *The Key to the Scriptures*, which they consider to be equally inspired. So in this category, the Bible is not the only authority but, in addition, there must be the writing of the founder of the cult, which is of equal authority.

Summary: These first five categories of attitudes toward the Scriptures can be categorized as false attitudes or false views of the Bible, because none of them are willing to accept the Bible alone as the final and supreme authority. In rationalism, the mind is supreme as the final authority. In mysticism, the experience is supreme as their final authority. In Romanism, the church is supreme and the final authority. In neo-orthodoxy, the individual's encounter is the supreme authority. Among the cults, the Bible plus the writings of the founder are supreme as the final authority.

---

[6] Question 5 on page 19

None of these first five attitudes can be classed as correct attitudes since they are not willing to accept the Bible alone as the final and supreme authority.[7]

6. Orthodoxy

The proper biblical attitude toward the Scriptures is orthodoxy. This is the attitude that the Bible alone is supreme and is the final authority. Orthodox believers will affirm that the Bible is the infallible Word of God. In the original writings, it is inspired and without error. The Bible is the final and only authority in all manners and matters of faith and practice. The Bible is true in everything that it affirms to be true.

Concerning rationalism, the mind or reason must be subservient to the Word of God. It is not the mind that judges the Scriptures, but the Scriptures judge the thoughts of the mind. Concerning the experience of mysticism, the Bible is the final judge of experience; experience cannot determine the truth of Scripture. Concerning Romanism, it is not the church that determines the meaning of the Bible; but rather, the Bible determines the proper place of the church. Concerning neo-orthodoxy, a man does not need a unique encounter before he can comprehend what is the Word of God in the Scriptures. The Bible is the Word of God. If one is a believer and has been regenerated by the Holy Spirit, he is by his very relationship to God receiving input or enlightenment from the Holy Spirit and can understand the Scriptures. Concerning the issue of the cults, the answer of orthodoxy is that the Bible—and the Bible alone—is supreme; the 66 books of the Scriptures are all that have been inspired by God in written form. Any other writing is the writing of a false prophet or false prophetess.

Those who hold to the supremacy of the Bible believe that knowledge is subject to the Bible; there is no "inner light" that adds revelation beyond the Bible. There is only the light of the Holy Spirit that illuminates the meaning of the Scriptures, but does not add any more revelation. There is no authority given to the church or to man beyond that which is given in the Scriptures themselves. [8]

---

[7] Question 6 on page 19

[8] Question 7 on page 19

C. THE WONDERS OF THE BIBLE

The wonders of the Bible can be seen in four specific ways: in its formation, its preservation, its subject matter, and in its influence.

1. Formation

The formation of the Bible shows its "diversity in unity." The 66 books of the Bible were written over a span of 1,600 years by about forty different men (some of these men, like Moses and Paul, wrote more than one book). The Bible was also written in three different languages: Hebrew, Greek, and Aramaic. During its formation it was written in various places, such as Israel, Babylon, Egypt, Greece, Rome, and Arabia (among others). Its writers also followed various occupations from shepherds to kings. Altogether, we know of at least eleven different occupations that were followed by the forty-odd authors of Scripture: kings, priests, prophets, soldiers, statesmen, shepherds, fishermen, tax-collectors, medical doctors, tent-makers, and farmers. The Bible also uses eight literary forms in its 66 books: narrative, biography, poetry, proverb, drama, sermons, letters (epistles), and psalms.

So one of the first wonders of the Bible is its wide diversity, yet with a complete unity. In spite of the fact that the Bible was written over a period of 1,600 years, by over 40 authors writing many different books in various languages, from different countries, using various literary forms, having widely differing occupations, we have a perfect unity and a perfect harmony. There is diversity, but it is within a unity, not a diversity which contradicts.

2. Preservation

A second wonder of the Bible is its preservation. The Bible has been well preserved as the text itself has remained intact. While the original manuscripts that were written by Moses or Isaiah or Paul or Peter are no longer in existence, what we do have are copies. Upon hearing that, many believe it is inevitable that mistakes have been made; that corruption of the text has occurred. We have indeed found a few mistakes in copying and some minor corruption of the text, but what is unique about the Scriptures is in the way God has preserved the copies. For example, take the Old Testament. Before the Dead Sea Scrolls were discovered, the oldest Hebrew manuscript we had was known as the Masoretic Text, which dated from about A.D. 1000. Critics would often charge that since our oldest manuscript was so late, that we could not possibly trust that the Old Testament was preserved properly from the original writings.

But in 1947, God allowed Hebrew manuscripts to be found which are now known as the Dead Sea Scrolls. These scrolls were written between the year 100 B.C. and A.D. 70, about 1,000 years before the Masoretic Text. As the archaeologists and textual critics began to compare the two sets of texts, only very minute differences were found. What was fascinating was that these differences never changed the meaning of any verse. For example, one text would say, "He went to Jerusalem," while the other would say, "He went unto Jerusalem." Any changes found were that slight and did not change the meaning of the text. The Hebrew text we have, verified by the Dead Sea Scrolls, shows that the original Old Testament text was very well preserved.

As for the New Testament, God has preserved numerous Greek manuscripts, and by virtue of comparing these many Greek texts, it is virtually possible to clearly determine what the original Greek New Testament said. It is truly a wonder that the text of the Bible has remained intact, in both the Hebrew Old Testament and the Greek New Testament.[9]

A second way that illustrates the preservation of the Scriptures is its indestructibility. In I Peter 1:24-25, God had promised that His Word would abide forever:

[24] For, all flesh is as grass, And all the glory thereof as the flower of grass. The grass withers, and the flower fails: [25] But the word of the Lord abides forever. And this is the word of good tidings which was preached unto you.

God has promised to preserve His Word from destruction, and indeed, there is ample evidence of this throughout history in that men have tried to destroy the Scriptures, but the Scriptures have been preserved. For example, the Roman Emperor Diocletian said, "The Christian religion is destroyed and the worship of the gods restored." Only ten years later, Emperor Constantine made Christianity the religion of the Roman Empire. Another example is that of the French philosopher Voltaire who stated, "Fifty years from now the world will hear no more about the Bible." But, exactly fifty years later, not only was the world still hearing about the Bible, but the Geneva Bible Society bought the very printing-press Voltaire used to spread his teachings against the Bible to print more Bibles. And So God again

---

[9] Question 8 on page 19

proved that His Word is indestructible by using the very thing that Voltaire used to try to destroy faith in the Bible to print even more Scriptures.

A third example of the Bible's indestructibility was the persecution of William Tyndale, an Englishman who translated the Bible into English. This was one of the very earliest translations, which preceded the King James Version. The Roman Catholic Church tried everything to destroy this English translation because they wanted to keep the Word of God away from the common knowledge of the people. They wanted to uphold the idea that the only valid Bible was the Latin version. Thus they tried desperately to destroy all the copies of the Tyndale Bible that could be found, until, it is believed, there was only one copy left. Today, the majority of Bibles are printed in English, so even those who were corrupt church leaders and tried to destroy the Word of God, found it could not be done.

Fourthly, Thomas Payne, one of this country's founding fathers, was an American philosopher who was a critic of the Scriptures. He began to write a series of diatribes against the Bible in which he said, "When I get through, there will not be five Bibles in America." While Thomas Payne did some good writing in defense of the American Revolution and American Independence, he was certainly wrong about the Scriptures. Today, the United States is the greatest producer of Bibles in English and many other languages.

These are clear evidences that the Bible remains indestructible by virtue of God's preserving power. The wonders of the Bible can be shown by its formation and by preservation.

3. Subject Matter

Including other holy books, the Scriptures are unique among all books in regard to subject matter. The subject matter is as diverse as the formation of the Bible itself. For example, the subjects of the Bible include the personality, unity, and the Trinity of God. The Bible speaks about mankind's origin and fall. It introduces the unique concept of the God-Man in the Person of *Yeshua* (Jesus) the Messiah. It deals with God's provision of salvation. The prophetic portions speak of the culmination of all history.

In spite of the diversity of the subject matter, there is still a unifying principle that all these things that do not seem to be connected are ultimately working toward the culmination of history for the glory of God. God will be glorified through all the various programs He has introduced to us in the Scriptures; such as, man's salvation, Israel's history, the Messianic Kingdom, and in many other ways.

Combining such great variety and diversity of subject matter to bring out the unifying principle of the glory of God shows the uniqueness and wonder of the Bible.

4. Influence

The Bible has had a tremendous influence upon both individuals and upon the course and history of nations. The Bible's influence on individuals affects true believers, but also unbelievers. The Bible has changed the lives of many individuals. It has inspired the writing of various classics and novels. It has inspired the paintings of some of the greatest artists in history. Indeed, it has had tremendous influence on individual men in the arts, sciences, and the humanities.

The Bible has also had an influence on nations. The concepts of cleanliness, legality, honor, and religiosity have all come from the influence of the Scriptures upon the nations that have embraced them. In fact, most of the law codes in the western world, both in Europe and the New World, were influenced by the law codes of the Scriptures.

But much more importantly, the Bible has had an influence upon individuals, bringing them to a personal relationship with God. It is through the Scriptures that people come to see that they are sinners and that they can do nothing about their sin on their own. The price of sin had to be paid, and *Yeshua* paid that price. The Bible has resulted in the regeneration and salvation of countless individuals.

D. THE SUPERNATURAL ORIGIN OF THE BIBLE

The final area of discussion concerning the nature of the Bible has to do with its supernatural origin. This can be clearly seen in ten different ways.

1. The Book of God

The supernatural origin of the Bible can be clearly seen in that it is the Book of God. The Bible is theocentric: God is the center of the Scriptures. Furthermore, while other holy books may talk about God, the Bible is still unique among books in the way it talks about God. The Bible presents God as different from the gods of other contemporary writers. Furthermore, the Bible presents God as monotheistic rather than the polytheistic gods, which were flagrant in the days when the Scriptures were written. Although later holy books such as the Koran and others also talk about monotheism, even here the Bible is unique in that only the Bible talks about the Trinity of this monotheism. Indeed, the Bible is the Book of God that presents Him as different from the ones depicted in all other holy books, whether contemporary or written later.[10]

2. The Problem of Sin

The supernatural origin of the Bible can be clearly seen in that the Bible alone presents the problem of sin and a cure for it that works. Only the Bible spells out sin for what it really is. Only the Bible presents a cure that truly and honestly works, as testified to by many who have experienced the supernatural working of the Scriptures in their lives.

3. Ethics and Morals

The supernatural origin of the Bible can be clearly seen in that it is unique in its ethics and morals. For example, the ethics and morals of the Bible are comprehensive in that they cover all areas of human conduct. They cover the areas of husband-wife relationships and parent-child relationships, proper conduct for employers and their employees, governments and their citizens, and states and the nation. It covers many spheres; such as, sexual, business, economic, and recreational. In all of these areas, the ethics and morals of the Scriptures are very comprehensive.

Furthermore, the ethics and morals of the Bible are unique in that the motives themselves are judged. The Bible does not merely deal with outward conformity to the standards of ethics and morals as other books do; it deals with the actual motivation involved.

Finally, the Bible provides the only basis for true ethical behavior; behavior based upon the recognition that God exists, and that He will judge every man according to his works.[11]

---

[10] Question 9 on page 20

[11] Question 10 on page 20

4. Continuity

A fourth evidence of the supernatural origin of Scriptures is its continuity. Although there are sixty-six books, written by forty-odd different writers, written over sixteen hundred years in three languages, coming from various professional backgrounds, and using different literary forms, there is a remarkable continuity and perfect harmony throughout. Most other "holy books" were written by just one author. For instance, the *Koran*—the holy book of Islam—was written by only one author, who was Mohammed. Most other "holy books," such as *The Book of Mormon* and similar writings, were written by only one author. Therefore, if only one author writes a book, continuity is easy to accomplish. But the continuity of Scripture is different, as it was put together by many writers, over many years, from various professions, and in various places, and using various literary methods.

5. Prophecies

The supernatural origin of the Scriptures is seen in its prophecies and their fulfillment. Other holy books contain prophecies, which are open to various interpretations, so that no matter how things turn out, they can still try to claim fulfillment. That is simply not the case with the Bible. The Bible contains very clear prophecies that tend to be very pointed and limited. Therefore, when the fulfillment comes, it is very exact. No other holy book can point to a lengthy series of prophecies followed by their perfect fulfillment. Yet in the Bible, that is exactly what we have. All other holy books, written by one author in a short period of time, cannot, of course, show prophecy and fulfillment. However, because of the uniqueness of the Bible's having been written over 1,600 years by forty different authors, one writer makes a prophecy, and many years later, another writer records the fulfillment of that prophecy.

6. Types and Antitypes

The supernatural origin of Scripture is seen in its types and anti-types. These demonstrate the unity between the Old and New Testaments. Although at least four hundred years transpired between the writing of the last Old Testament book and the writing of the first New Testament book, and we move from the Hebrew language of the Old Testament to the Greek language of the New Testament, still the typologies of the Old Testament have a clear and obvious fulfillment in the antitypes of the New Testament. There is clear unity of the Old and New

Testaments in spite of the diversity of language and centuries of separation between them.[12]

7. Literary Value

A seventh evidence for the supernatural origin of the Bible is its literary form. The Bible as literature is paramount. Even unbelievers, who are themselves literary critics, recognize the literary uniqueness of the Scriptures. In contemporary literature, there is simply no comparison to that of the Bible.[13]

8. Absence of Prejudice

The Bible is unprejudiced in the way it portrays its heroes. Most of the other holy books never report the shortcomings of their heroes. Their heroes were always just that: heroes. But the Bible points out the shortcomings and failures of its heroes as well as their best qualities. For example, the Scriptures called King David "a man after God's own heart." They viewed him as a hero, a great warrior, and one who gained victory by use of his military might and abilities. At the same time, the same Bible points out David's failures. His failure in dealing properly with his son Absalom in a father-son relationship is clearly reported. The Bible also reported David's adultery and his responsibility in the death of Bathsheba's husband. The Bible is, indeed, unprejudiced, pointing to the shortcomings and failures of its heroes.[14]

9. Scientific Accuracy

A ninth evidence for the supernatural origin of the Bible is the relationship of the Bible to science. The Bible itself is not a book on science. Whenever it touches on science though, it has always proved itself to be absolutely accurate. The Bible has never had to be revised based upon the proven facts of science, while science itself had to continuously be revised as new discoveries have been made. As far as proven facts of science are concerned, not one has ever proven that the Scriptures

---

[12] Question 11 on page 20

[13] Question 12 on page 20

[14] Question 13 on page 20

are wrong. So while the Bible is not a scientific book, where it does touch on science it has been proven to be absolutely accurate and without error.

10. Enduring Freshness

The supernatural origin of the Bible is seen in its enduring freshness. It is read and reread like no other book. This author can say, "I have lost count of how often I have read through the Bible since I became a believer at the age of thirteen. I have read the Bible many times, over and over again, and I have never found myself bored. I cannot stand to read most books even a second time, because I already know the plot and know what will happen. So I simply do not read a book a second time. But there is a difference with the Bible. I have reread it and reread it, and because it contains an enduring freshness, it continually retains my interest."[15]

    Louis Sperry Chafer, the founder of Dallas Theological Seminary, once said: "The Bible is not a book man could write if he would. And the Bible is not a book man would write if he could."[16]

---

[15] Question 14 on page 20

[16] Study Suggestion 2 on page 20

E. Questions and Study Suggestions

Question 1: Have you had an experience similar to Peter's? In this context, discuss the following statement with your fellow students: "Doubt is often on the human plane or perspective, but when your heart opens to God's truth, it rises above the human plane and into that sovereign relationship."

Suggestion 1 (to the study group leaders): It is recommended that the first meeting goes through to point 5 of the attitudes towards the Bible. The following meeting goes into part 6. OR have your students' homework be through 5 and then go through 6 together in class.

Question 2: Today, this is prevalent in some cultures. Some who hold to their views do not know how to label them. Have you or someone you've talked to expressed how the human mind is the final judge? Do you think God values the human minds? Who created the human mind?

Question 3: What is false mysticism? What is true mysticism? Can your experiences validate Scripture? Does Scripture ask to be validated by experience? Do you know Scripture and the importance of knowing Scripture in order for the Holy Spirit to illuminate your mind?

Question 4: Have you been taught about Romanism? Or experienced Romanism or know someone who has? From what you know about the unique terms of the Bible verified in use and context from God's Word, does God hold the Roman church as supreme over the Bible?

Question 5: Some say that God's Word means different things to different people. Others think that one individual at different points in life might view the same passage differently. How would you respond to this belief?

Question 6: Have you or someone you know studied from or followed a cult-based belief system?

Question 7: Of all five categories of false attitudes, which of them have you struggled with either within your own heart or in discussion with people you know? Is there a point of clarity in your mind now in response to those previous thoughts?

Question 8: Sometimes, people will ask, "How do we know we have the original Scriptures? How do we know we have the Bible as it was originally written?" How will you answer this question going forward after this study?

Question 9: What holy book are you familiar with? What is your relationship with the Bible? Do you view the Bible as a book about God or a book to understand people or yourself?

Question 10: Is man the solution, or is God the solution? Clarify what you are thinking with the uniqueness of the Bible.

Question 11: Define 'types' and 'antitypes'.

Question 12: Does accepting the Bible as unique literature agree completely with how God represents His Word? Is there more to true belief than literary acceptance?

Question 13: If the Bible presents the problem of sin and the cure for sin, what is the benefit or result of God being unprejudiced in pointing out the short comings and failures of these heroes?

Question 14: Discuss how you have personally experienced the freshness of the Bible.

Suggestion 2: Take the online test for this section of the study of the Word of God found on http://ariel.org/come-and-see.htm under "The Nature of the Bible (030)," quiz.

Chapter III

The Bible and Divine Revelation

What do we mean by the term "revelation?" It should be pointed out at the outset that we do not mean the *book* of Revelation, rather, we mean God's *act* of revelation as He reveals Himself through the Holy Scriptures.

This English word is a translation of the Greek word ἀποκάλυψις (*apokalupsis*) which means "the unveiling" or "uncovering." It refers to a divine act of communicating (unveiling) to man what otherwise could not and would be known, as God can only be known through the revelation of Himself. God is the incomprehensible One, so it is impossible ever to have a perfect knowledge of God.[17]

God can be known only because He reveals Himself. The nature of God is such that man, on his own, cannot discover God. When a Soviet astronaut came back from one of the first trips into space, he stated that he saw no evidence of God out there and, therefore, concluded that communist atheism was absolutely correct. But just because he could not see God in space does not mean that God does not exist; God has other ways of revealing Himself. In fact, someone else made a statement that, if the astronaut had stepped out of his spaceship, he would have seen God rather quickly.

God is simply incomprehensible. A good illustration of this is Job 11:7, where we read: *Can you by searching find out God? Can you find out the Almighty unto perfection?* The answer to that, of course, is "No."

---

[17] Suggestion 1 on page 37

The next question to consider is how God chose to reveal Himself to us. What are the modes of revelation? We can sub-divide this into two major categories: general revelation and special revelation.

A. GENERAL REVELATION

Under this heading, we want to discuss three things. First, the nature of general revelation; second, the means of general revelation; and third, the limitations of general revelation.

1. The Nature of General Revelation

Theologians refer to general revelation as *revelatio realis*. This is a Latin term that means either "the reality of revelation" or "the revelation of real things." In more down-to-earth terms it is "revelation embodied in things." General revelation has been defined as "the embodiment of divine thought in the phenomenon of nature, in the fact or experience of history, and the general constitution of the human mind." General revelation is basically God's revelation through nature, history, and human experience (i.e. through the very constitution of a human being). By its very nature then, general revelation is something that is available to all and appears to all men. Its object is to supply man's need for religious answers and to persuade the individual soul to seek after a personal God. Thus, it is given and available to everyone.

Again, general revelation is the revelation by which God reveals Himself to all men. Its emphasis is to get man to begin searching for God in a real and personal way.

2. The Means of General Revelation

There are four means whereby general revelation is made known. The first and primary means is that of **nature**. God reveals Himself to all people in general through nature. Psalm 19:1-6 tells us that through nature God has revealed His glory in the concept of creation. Isaiah 40:12-14 and 26 show that through nature God has revealed His own individuality and separateness from other gods made by human hands. Acts 14:14-17 states that man can learn about the goodness of God through nature. In Romans 1:19-20, man can learn about God's power and divinity through nature. So one way God has revealed Himself by means of general revelation is through nature, in order that man can learn about His glory, individuality, goodness, power, and divinity.

A second way by which God reveals Himself is through **providence**. This is God's revelation through history. History is the execution of the divine program of the ages in all of its details. So for example, according to Job 38:22-23, man can learn about the providence of God when suddenly there is snow in the day of battle and the future history of armies and nations can turn upon its arrival from the sky. It was by means of snow that Napoleon was forced to withdraw from Russia. It was also by means of snow that the Nazis were forced to retreat from Russia. A person observing history should be able to see that the coming of certain types of weather at certain crucial points in time was no mere fluke, but was God's providence being worked out in history.

Psalm 75:6-7 says that God is in control of who ascends the thrones of the world. So the reason why certain key people are placed in positions of authority at certain crucial points in history is in the providence of God. Whereas, on the one hand, we had a Hitler in Berlin, it was no mere quirk of history that at the same time there was a Stalin in Moscow or a Churchill in London or a Roosevelt in Washington D.C. Through the combined efforts of these men, they were able to defeat Hitler. So God is in control of who ascends the thrones of human government, and an observer of history could learn things about the providence of God by this means of general revelation.

Acts 17:26 teaches that the boundaries of peoples and nations are determined by God's providence. In Deuteronomy 32:8-9, the way history develops is often based upon God's providence in the experience of the people of Israel. Romans 8:28 says that God's providence works out in the life of the believer as He works all things together for good to those He calls.

The second means of general revelation then is providence, which is also available to all men. If people really look upon history in the way they should, they will learn certain things about God and His control and shaping of nations and ages.[18]

The third means of general revelation is **preservation**. People should learn from the way God has chosen to preserve the universe and the human race. In Acts 17:28, we see human preservation, while in Colossians 1:17 and Hebrews 1:3,

---

[18] Suggestion 2 on page 37

there is universal preservation. It is God's preservation, the "atomic glue" scientists speak about, that holds the universe together. And if any scientist would really contemplate this, he could, if he were open to it, learn certain truths about God. This, too, is part of general revelation, another way that God has revealed Himself to all men.

The fourth means of general revelation is **conscience**. God has revealed to all men certain things which are true by means of their conscience. "Conscience" is the revelation of the existence of absolute law. Some philosophers have recognized this in their writings, like Immanuel Kant who argued that moral requirements are based on a standard of rationality that he dubbed the "Categorical Imperative." By stating this, he recognized the existence of an absolute law.

Romans 2:14-15 says, *They show that the work of the law is written on their hearts, while their conscience also bears witness...,* teaching that even those people who did not have a clear revelation of God through specific laws kept certain laws because they recognized the existence of an absolute law. There are certain laws, such as those relating to murder and stealing, for example, which are common throughout the world. No matter how pagan a tribe might be, or how cultured a nation might be, there are certain laws which are common to them all. Once again this shows God's general revelation through conscience and is a part of all men.

These are the four means of general revelation: through nature, through providence, through preservation, and through conscience. These are things which are common to all men in general, which is why it is called *general* revelation. People who are open to spiritual things can certainly learn certain truths about God from these four means of general revelation.

3. The Limitations of General Revelation

While general revelation is sufficient to teach man general things about God so that he is prompted to start seeking a personal God, it is insufficient to lead him to salvation. It provides man with only a limited knowledge. It does not give him enough to be saved. What a man needs to believe in order to be saved is the gospel: that *Yeshua* died for his sins, was buried, and rose again from the dead. General revelation will not reveal that truth to any individual. General revelation can cause a person to begin seeking after truth which will eventually bring him to a place where he will hear the gospel. However, it will never produce enough revelation to cause a man to be saved; in that sense, it is limited.

In Acts 17:23, we read: *For as I passed along and observed the objects of your worship, I found also an altar with this inscription: TO AN UNKNOWN GOD. What therefore ye worship in ignorance, this I set forth unto you.* Through general revelation, the Greeks were able to determine that, besides the many gods they already worshiped, there had to be a God about whom they did not know. That much general revelation revealed to them; but who this unknown God is, general revelation could not tell them. That had to come by means of a more special revelation, which in this passage came to them through the Apostle Paul. So Acts 17:23 illustrates the possible extent of general revelation. General revelation in and of itself was never enough to bring mankind to saving faith. And So Paul writes that the gospel is hidden and cannot become available through general revelation. Therefore, in Ephesians 3:8-9, he writes these words:

⁸ Unto me, who am less than the least of all saints, was this grace given, to preach unto the Gentiles the unsearchable riches of Messiah; ⁹ and to make all men see what is the dispensation of the mystery which for ages has been hid in God who created all things…

According to I Corinthians 15:1-4, the gospel message is necessary for salvation. While general revelation could, by itself, cause a man to start searching, which in turn would lead him to find the gospel, general revelation by itself is not sufficient for salvation.

On the other hand, it is sufficient to condemn. In Romans 1:20, Paul emphasized this particular truth when he wrote: *For the invisible things of him since the creation of the world are clearly seen, being perceived through the things that are made, even his everlasting power and divinity; that they may be without excuse.* Paul explains that people could learn certain general truths about God by general revelation. Those of whom the apostle speaks did not live up to the light that was available to them through general revelation, and, for that very reason, they were "without excuse." Thus we see that general revelation is sufficient to condemn. Therefore, if a pagan dies without believing, when he stands before the Great White Throne judgment seat, he will not be able to use the excuse, "I never heard the gospel." God will show him that there was truth available through general revelation in nature, providence, preservation, and conscience; and had he lived up to the light available, God would have made sure he was given more light. But the fact that he did not live up to the light that he did have through general revelation means that he would not have accepted any further light, had it come to him.

This is one explanation of how a person born and raised in the Midwest, perhaps in Kansas or Missouri, suddenly has a tremendous burden to go to a remote tribe in

Africa or South America that very few people have heard about. He has this burden because there are people among these tribes who are living up to the light they have, and if they are given more light, they will believe. So God sends someone to share the gospel with them. If a person dies without ever hearing about *Yeshua* the Messiah, it means he would not have believed even if he had heard the gospel. The proof of it is that he had not lived up to the light he did have. So at the Great White Throne judgment, general revelation will be sufficient to condemn.

To summarize this section, one of the modes of divine revelation is general revelation. This is the revelation by which God reveals Himself generally to all men. We can learn a lot of things about God through general revelation, but it has the limitation that no one will receive the content of the gospel through it. Therefore, it is sufficient to condemn, but it is insufficient to save.[19]

B. SPECIAL REVELATION

The second main type of revelation, and the one we are most concerned with in our study of the Word of God, is special revelation. In dealing with this subject, we will discuss three main aspects: the nature, the necessity, and the means of special revelation.

1. The Nature of Special Revelation

Theologically, the nature of special revelation is referred to as *revelatio verbalis*, which means "revelation embodied in words." General revelation is embodied in things, but special revelation is embodied in words. In special revelation, God makes Himself known at specific times, through specific people, and in specific ways.

2. The Necessity of Special Revelation

There are four reasons why special revelation is necessary. First, it is necessary in order to correctly interpret the truths which come from general revelation.

---

[19] Suggestion 3 on page 37

Second, it is necessary to illuminate men so that they can read God in nature correctly and not misinterpret nature and fall into idolatry as the people Paul wrote about in Romans 1:20-25:

> [20] *For the invisible things of him since the creation of the world are clearly seen, being perceived through the things that are made, even his everlasting power and divinity; that they may be without excuse:* [21] *because that, knowing God, they glorified him not as God, neither gave thanks; but became vain in their reasonings, and their senseless heart was darkened.* [22] *Professing themselves to be wise, they became fools,* [23] *and changed the glory of the incorruptible God for the likeness of an image of corruptible man, and of birds, and four-footed beasts, and creeping things.* [24] *wherefore God gave them up in the lusts of their hearts unto uncleanness, that their bodies should be dishonored among themselves:* [25] *for that they exchanged the truth of God for a lie, and worshipped and served the creature rather than the Creator, who is blessed for ever. Amen.*

Third, special revelation is necessary to furnish man with a revelation of salvation. Again, general revelation can never provide the content of the gospel. It was insufficient to save, so special revelation was necessary to furnish man with a revelation of salvation.

Fourth, special revelation is necessary to harmonize the seeming contradictions in general revelation. For instance, the goodness of God is seen through the periodic rains that cause the seed to grow, yet the severity of God is seen by destructive rains that destroy the growing plants and wheat. This seems to contradict the nature of God. It is impossible to harmonize these truths from general revelation alone, but this is possible through special revelation.[20]

3. The Means of Special Revelation

The means of special revelation is summarized by Hebrews 1:1-2:

> [1] *God, having of old time spoken unto the fathers in the prophets by divers portions and in divers manners,* [2] *has at the end of these days spoken unto us in his Son...*

---

[20] Question 1 on page 37

This passage of Scripture points out that God has revealed Himself in a number of different means or ways throughout biblical history using special revelation. What are these various ways that the writer of Hebrews refers to when he writes about different ways of special revelation? Altogether, there are six different means of special revelation.

a. Theophanies

The first means of special revelation is through what theologians call theophanies. This term comes from two Greek words which mean "the appearance of God." It emphasizes the appearance of God in some visible way where He chose to reveal Himself to man.

In the Old Testament, this came primarily in two forms. The first form the Jewish rabbis referred to as the *Shechinah* Glory. This was a visible manifestation of God's presence where the omnipresence of God took on a localized form and the normally invisible God became visible. God actually took on this visible, localized form in many ways and in many times throughout the history of Scripture in order to give special revelation. The *Shechinah* primarily came in the form of light or fire or cloud or a combination of these things.

The second major form of a theophany was the Angel of Jehovah. What is very evident is that throughout the pages of the Old Testament, whenever the Angel of the Lord—the Angel of Jehovah—appeared, it was never a common, ordinary angel, but rather, it was always the Second Person of the Trinity appearing in angelic form.

Thus, one means of special revelation was by way of theophanies, the appearance of God in a visible form, either by means of the *Shechinah* Glory or by means of the Angel of the Lord.

b. Miracles

A second means of special revelation is by miracles. Miracles in Scripture are special revelations from God.

(1) The Definition of Miracles

A simple definition of a miracle is that it is an unusual event that accompli-shes a useful work in revealing the presence and the power of God. A more detailed definition of a miracle reads like this: An event in nature so extraordinary in itself, and so coinciding with a prophecy or a command of a spiritual leader or teacher, as to fully warrant a conviction that God has wrought it with the design of certifying this teacher or leader that he has been commissioned by God.

Basically, a miracle is an extraordinary event that is inexplicable in terms of ordinary, natural facts.

(2) The Nature of Miracles

The nature of miracles is seen in four ways. First, miracles are distinct from providence. In providence, people do not necessarily acknowledge God, but in a miracle, even unbelievers acknowledge that something supernatural has occurred. For instance, in Acts 3:1-4:22, when the miracle of the healing of the lame beggar occurred, even unbelievers acknowledged it to be the work of God (Acts 4:14-16, 21-22). In Acts 14:8-18, when a cripple was healed, even unbelievers acknowledged this to be a work of God (vv. 8-12). A miracle, then, is distinct from providence in that even unbelievers will acknowledge its supernatural character.

Second, the nature of a miracle is that it is distinct from answered prayer, which does not constitute a sign. While on one hand, a miracle could result from an answered prayer, it is nevertheless distinct from the answered prayer itself in that miracles can come separately from prayer.

Third, miracles do not break natural laws; they are the result of supernatural power that supersedes these laws.

Fourth, the nature of a miracle has a supernatural character, disclosing divine power. That is the point which had clearly made an impression upon Nicodemus in John 3:2, where we read: *The same came to Yeshua by night, and said unto Him, Rabbi, we know that You are a teacher come from God, for no one can do these signs that You do except God be with him.* As an unbeliever, Nicodemus had to acknowledge that miracles had taken place, and he recognized that they disclosed supernatural divine power.

(3) Two Types of Miracles

The first type of miracle is when natural law is intensified, such as in the Noahic Flood. Floods are not uncommon and occur all the time, but with the Noahic Flood there was an intensification of natural law in that it was a worldwide flood.

The other type of miracle is when the participation of nature is totally excluded. This happened, for example, when Moses brought water from a rock and when people were raised from the dead. In no way can it be said that nature cooperated with God in these things.

(4) The Facets of Miracles

There are three facets of miracles. First and foremost, they are extraordinary works of God in that they show the exercise of His supernatural and divine power. This power produces amazement, but not necessarily fear, as seen in Exodus 14:13 and Luke 9:43 where those watching marveled at the miracles of God.

Second, miracles were worked through chosen men, but the power was recognized to be from God. God worked miracles through whomever He chose, but the observers recognized it to be His power. We see this in Acts 2:22 and 19:11 where the miracles of Peter and Paul where credited to God.

The third facet of miracles is that they are revelatory events. They include the unveiling of some type of divine truth.

(5) The Frequency of Miracles

We are often told in many circles that there are always miracles throughout the Bible and, therefore, there should always be miracles today; but that, too, is a fallacy.

Actually, throughout the entire history of the Bible, which covered nearly four thousand years, there were only three major periods of miracles. The first period was that of the Exodus and the Wilderness Wanderings, which lasted only forty years. The second is the period of Elijah and Elisha. The third period of miracles is that of the Messiah and the apostles. Generally speaking, miracles did not happen all the time. If miracles were common elements of the human experience, they would no longer be miraculous. The nature of miracles is the concept of the extraordinary, the concept of the unusual, something that does not occur on a regular basis.

(6) The Vocabulary of Miracles

There are four different words used for the concept of miracles, each emphasizing a distinctive nature. The first word is τέρας (*teras*, Acts 2:22), and it means "a wonder." It emphasizes that a miracle is that which awakens wonder. A second Greek word is δύναμις (*dunamis*, Acts 19:11) which means "power," and it emphasizes a miracle as something that was wrought by divine power. A third Greek word is ἔργον (*ergon*, Acts 13:31) which means "work," and it emphasizes miracles as accomplishing a practical, useful, and beneficial end. The fourth word is σημεῖον (*seimeion*, Act 4:16), meaning "sign." It emphasizes the miracle as a sign which authenticates the messenger and his message as being from God.

(7) The Purpose of Miracles

There are three specific reasons why miracles occurred. First, they happened to affirm new revelation from God as shown in Matthew 12:28. This is also the point made in II Corinthians 12:12 where Paul reminds the Corinthians of the signs, wonders, and miracles he did to authenticate his ministry. These miracles affirmed the new message of the gospel and the start of God's new revelation through the church.

A second purpose is to affirm doctrine. However, doctrine and miracles must be in unity with each other. A doctrine can stand alone, but miracles cannot stand alone because Satan can also produce miracles. This is where people get caught up into movements where they never mature or never get saved because they assume that the existence of the supernatural automatically means it is of God. Nothing can be farther from the truth, for Satan himself can perform miracles. For example, Matthew 7:22-23 states that many will come to *Yeshua* and say:

> [22] *... Lord, Lord, did we not prophesy by your name, and by your name cast out demons, and by your name do many mighty works?* [23] *And then He will say to them: I never knew you: depart from me, ye that work iniquity.*

This is an example of miracles, but not doctrine. First Corinthians 4:6 tells us not to *go beyond the things which are written*. Miracles must conform to the things written in Scripture (doctrine) for their authentication, otherwise they may be false, demonic miracles. Miracles do not prove doctrine, rather the inverse is true: doctrine authenticates the miracle. That is why every miracle must be tested by the Word of God, to make sure it is of God, not of Satan.[21]

The third purpose of miracles is to manifest the power of God.[22]

c. Direct Communication

A third means of special revelation is by direct communication. This was limited to the prophets, as the very nature of a prophet was one who received direct revelation from God. In Numbers 12:5-8, this is brought out quite strongly:

> [5] *And Jehovah came down in a pillar of cloud, and stood at the door of the Tent, and called Aaron and Miriam; and they both came forth.* [6] *And he said, Hear now my words: if there be a prophet among you, I Jehovah will make*

---

[21] Suggestion 4 on page 37

[22] Question 2 on page 37

myself known unto him in a vision, I will speak with him in a dream. [7] *My servant Moses is not so; he is faithful in all my house:* [8] *with him will I speak mouth to mouth, even manifestly, and not in dark speeches; and the form of Jehovah shall he behold: wherefore then were ye not afraid to speak against my servant, against Moses?*

The emphasis here is that those who receive direct communication are going to be the prophets of God. The same truth is reemphasized in I Samuel 28:6, which reads: *And when Saul inquired of Jehovah, Jehovah answered him not, neither by dreams, nor by Urim, nor by prophets.* The prophets were the ones who were receiving direct communication and revelation. This came in seven different ways.

The first form was *mouth to mouth*, as in the case of Moses in Numbers 12:7-8. This was also called *face to face* in Deuteronomy 34:10, and this was an experience unique to Moses.

The second form was by means of an audible voice, where God spoke audibly to the individual from Heaven. This is how it was with Adam in Genesis 2:16, and with both Adam and Eve in Genesis 3:8-19. He also spoke this way to Cain in Genesis 4:6-15, to Noah in Genesis 9:1-17, to the multitude of Israel at Sinai in Exodus 19:9, 16 and Deuteronomy 5:4-5, to Samuel in I Samuel 3:4-15, to Paul in Acts 9:4, and to Peter in Acts 10:19. These are all examples of where God spoke with an audible voice.

The third form was by the casting of lots. God communicated directly by this method, to which Joshua 14:1-2 attests. God decided and then communicated which tribe would get which part of the territory by the casting of lots. Likewise, this method was the way the twenty-four courses of priests were selected (I Chron. 24:1-31), the way it was decided who would live in Jerusalem (Neh. 11:1). In Jonah 1:7, this was the way it was discovered that Jonah was the guilty party.

The fourth form was by the *Urim and Thummim*. This was the name given to the twelve stones upon the breastplate of the High Priest, representing the twelve tribes. The name means "lights and "perfections." God was able to communicate directly by answering questions requiring only a yes or no answer. If the answer was "Yes," the stones would light up. If the answer was "No," they would not light up. We see this in the following passages:

1) In Exodus 28:30 and Leviticus 8:8, this was part of Israel's worship.

2) Deuteronomy 33:8 gives us the principle of usage.

3) In Numbers 27:21, we see it used by Joshua.

4) In Joshua 7:16-21, it helped discover that it was Achan's sin which brought about Israel's defeat at Ai.

5) In Judges 20:26-28, it was used to decide the war against the Benjaminites.

6) It was used again in I Samuel 10:20-24 to make Saul king.

7) The *Urim and Thummim* was the way in which Jonathan was found out (I Sam. 14:36-42).

8) David used it to determine God's will (I Sam. 23:9-12; 30:7-8).

9) In I Samuel 28:6, Saul attempted to use it, but failed.

So it is clear in Scripture that this was the way God communicated directly up until the Babylonian Captivity. Somehow, the *Urim and Thummim* were destroyed in the destruction of Jerusalem in 586 B.C. Ezra 2:62-63 and Nehemiah 7:64-65 are the last references to these objects in the Scriptures.

The fifth form of direct communication happened by means of dreams. A few examples are:

1) Genesis 20:3-7, in the case of Abimelech;

2) Genesis 28:12-16, it was how God communicated with Jacob.

3) Genesis 31:24, it was how God communicated with Laban.

4) Genesis 37:5-9, it was how God communicated with Joseph.

5) Genesis 40:1-23, God also revealed Himself to the Egyptian baker and butler through dreams.

6) Genesis 41:1-36, to Pharaoh;

7) Judges 7:13-14, concerning the Midianites;

8) I Kings 3:5, to Solomon;

9) Daniel 2 and 7:1-2, to Nebuchadnezzar;

10) Matthew 1:20; 2:13, 19, to Joseph, the step-father of *Yeshua*.

In all these cases, God revealed Himself by means of dreams.

The sixth form of direct communication by God was through visions. Sometimes God gave a vision, rather than a dream. That is the way it was with Abraham in Genesis 15:1 and with Isaiah in Isaiah 6:1—13 when he was called to be a prophet. God gave visions to Ezekiel in Ezekiel 1—3 and 8—11 where he saw the fall of Jerusalem, to Daniel in Daniel 2:19 to interpret Nebuchadnezzar's dream, and to Amos in Amos 7—9.

The seventh and final form of direct communication was through inner illumination as mentioned in II Peter 1:21.

d. Angels

A fourth major means of giving special revelation was by means of angels. The Law of Moses, for example, came by means of angels according to Acts 7:53 and Galatians 3:19. It was angels who revealed the birth of Messiah to the shepherds in Luke 2:10 and 13. Angels were also used to reveal things to Daniel in Daniel 9:20-21 and 10:10-21. So clearly, God chose to reveal Himself at times through angels as the means of special revelation.

e. Incarnation

The fifth means of special revelation was by the Incarnation. When God became a man by means of the God-Man, He revealed Himself even further in the person of *Yeshua*. Everything that is true about the divine nature of the Father is also true of the Son.

Many Scriptures teach that the Incarnation became a very special means, a very special form, of special revelation. In Matthew 11:27, the Son revealed the Father. In John 1:14 and 18, *Yeshua* came to reveal the glory of the Father. In John 14:8-9, one of His disciples asked Him to show them the Father, and *Yeshua* answered, "If you have seen Me, you have seen the Father." Colossians 2:9 states that *all the fullness of the Godhead* indwelt bodily in the Son. According to I John 1:1-4, to see *Yeshua* meant to see God; to see *Yeshua's* work was to see the work of God; to hear *Yeshua's* teaching was to hear the very words of God. In Hebrews 1:1-2, the writer states that God has revealed Himself in various ways and in various forms throughout history, but has, in these last days, revealed Himself to us by means of His Son.

f. Scriptures

The sixth and last means of special revelation is by the Scriptures. The Scriptures are the Word of God, the written revelation of God, by which one can rightfully interpret all the other forms of revelation. By means of Scripture, it is possible to rightly interpret everything revealed through general revelation. By means of Scripture, it is possible to correctly interpret the other five forms of special revelation. It is by means of Scripture that one can interpret theophanies. It is by means of Scripture that one can interpret miracles and be able to know how far a miracle can go. In this way, the Scriptures are more important than any miracle, for in Luke 16:31, Abraham said to the rich man: *If they hear not Moses and the prophets, neither will they be persuaded, if one rise from the dead.*

Resurrection from the dead is a stupendous miracle, but by itself, it is insufficient to bring one to faith. Miracles will fail to convince if the Scriptures are not believed. By means of Scripture, it is possible to determine which miracles are true and which are false. By means of Scripture, it is known that Satan can duplicate many of God's miracles. By means of Scripture, it is known that miracles are not a common event, but an unusual event. Also by means of Scripture, one can rightfully interpret the various forms of direct communication. By means of Scripture, it is possible to interpret the revelations that were given by angels. By means of Scripture, one can fully understand what the Incarnation was about and how to rightfully interpret the revelation received from the Incarnation. By far, the Scriptures are the most important of the six different modes of special revelation for man today.

While the Scriptures are able to provide partial knowledge of God, it is all that God has chosen to let us know for now, according to Deuteronomy 29:29. The primary goal of the Scriptures is unto redemption, according to II Timothy 3:15. On this score, it provides what general revelation fails to provide: the content of the gospel.[23]

The Scriptures are the sufficient revelation of God, though they are not the exhaustive revelation. Romans 8:18 states that, in the future glory, further revelation will be given. First Corinthians 13:12 teaches that there will be future knowledge to be gained, and Jude 3 tells us that final revelation will come only in the glorified state. For now, in the present state, Scripture is the final revelation. Therefore, Paul admonishes believers *not to go beyond the things which are written,* in I Corinthians 4:6. It is by the *written* Word of God that the truth or error of everything with which we are confronted in spiritual warfare can be determined. It is revelation by means of words, according to I Thessalonians 2:13. It is the Scriptures that contain the *Thus says the Lord.*

---

[23] Suggestion 5 on page 37

C. Progressive Revelation

Thus far we have talked about general revelation and special revelation, because these are the two main types of revelation. But now, we need to talk about a third element, which theologically is referred to as progressive revelation.

Progressive revelation is not a third mode or type of revelation; rather it explains the revelation that came through the Scriptures. All revelation was not given at one time. God did not choose to reveal everything He wanted us to know all at once. So the Bible, with its sixty-six books, was given to us over some sixteen hundred years. Each piece of revelation was a step, and each step was a progression in the unfolding of God's plan and purpose. However, it should be understood that each step in the unfolding of God's plan and purpose was perfect in itself. Each step also combined to produce a flawless and complete whole. When God revealed truth up to a certain point, it was a complete revelation in itself, although there was more to be revealed later.

This is what is meant by progressive revelation. God did not reveal everything all at once, but as He put the Scriptures together, He took a period of sixteen-hundred years to do so. Therefore, the revelation was not instantaneous, it was progressive. It should also be noted that progressive revelation is the biblical basis for dispensationalism, because each dispensation required the giving of a new revelation. Dispensational changes actually came with more revelation, as revelation progressed. This subject is a bigger part of Bibliology which we will be dealing with later in this book.

There is general revelation and there is special revelation, with the primary form of special revelation being the written Word of God: the Scriptures. We will close this chapter with the admonition of Paul that the Bible is the final authority, so one must be careful *not to go beyond the things which are written.*[24]

---

[24] Suggestion 6 on page 37

D. Questions and Study Suggestions

Suggestion 1: With this definition in mind, discuss with your fellow students why man, on his own, cannot discover God. Discuss terms like "finite man" and "infinite God."

Suggestion 2: Discuss how this teaching about providence might alter one's thoughts on current events.

Suggestion 3: Journal through the 'insufficient for salvation' passages and the 'sufficient for condemnation' passages, noting your thoughts as you read these truths. Hold these truths about general revelation in focus as you further study God's Word. Can you witness this truth going forward in a world that wants people to go to Heaven outside of accepting the gospel?

Question 1: Have you asked questions of why God would allow bad things to happen? How does the distinction between general revelation and special revelation encourage you to pursue a greater understanding of the study of Bibliology?

Suggestion 4: Discuss a few examples of satanic miracles found in the Bible.

Question 2: Based on the attitudes toward the Bible, does this verify one specific attitude you looked at in the last chapter?

Suggestion 5: Look up II Timothy 3:15. In this context, discuss Mark 16:15 and the importance of Bible translations.

Suggestion 6: Take the online test for this section of the study of the Word of God found on http://ariel.org/come-and-see.htm under "The Bible and Divine Revelation (034)," quiz.

The Word of God

Chapter IV

The Inspiration of the Scriptures

We now come to the third major division of Bibliology, which is the inspiration of the Scriptures. Later on, we will distinguish between revelation and inspiration more clearly. For the time being, it is enough to note that while revelation has to do with the receiving of the truth, inspiration has to do with the recording of the truth.

A. Definition

Biblical inspiration can be defined as "God's superintendence of the human authors so that, using their own individual personality, they composed and recorded without error His revelation to man in the words of the original autographs." With this definition in mind, there are three ramifications that can be derived.

1. God's Superintendence

"God's superintendence" means that God superintended, but He did not dictate the writings. Obviously, there are certain portions of the Scriptures that God did dictate, and these were written down word-for-word. For example, the Ten Commandments and many of the other commandments of the Law of Moses were dictated word-for-word from God's mouth to Moses' ears; Moses then recorded it on the parchments that he had in front of him. But most of the Bible was not dictated word-for-word. Instead, God chose to superintend the writers. By superintending the writers, He was able to carefully control what was being written without having to dictate. So the end product still turned out exactly the way He wanted it to.

2. Human Authors

God used human authors and their individual styles. Obviously, if God simply dictated the Scriptures word-for-word, the entire Bible would sound the same. But, if you go from author to author, it is not the same. Each of the forty authors of the sixty-six books of the Bible used his own individual style; for example, Paul wrote in a different style from Peter; Moses wrote in a different style from Joshua. But because of God's superintendence and His control over these writers, He was able to allow them to use their own individual style of writing. And they still produced word-for-word exactly what God wanted them to produce.

3. Inerrancy

Inerrancy means that, when these original writings were produced, they were without error. For example: when Moses finished writing his five books, they were totally inspired by God, and there was no error in any one of them, and when Joshua was inspired to write his book, he wrote it without error. So the inspiration of the Scriptures pertains only to the original autographs of the Scriptures.

This does not mean that the copies of Scripture were inspired. Today, there is more than one manuscript of the various books of the Bible. There are a number of Hebrew copies and even a greater number of Greek copies, and there are slight discrepancies in words and word order between one manuscript and another, because these manuscripts were only copies. Unfortunately, copies were subject to some degree of human error, but the verbally inspired originals were without error. So it should be remembered that the copies were not inspired.

Translations of Scripture are not inspired either. In translating from one language to another, every translation may have a point of error to some degree. The King James Version, the American Standard Version, and the New American Standard have errors. Fortunately, the errors are never that significant, and it is possible to clearly know what the original writings were trying to say. Thus, translations of the original writings were not inspired nor necessarily without error.

4. God's Revelation

God so directed the human authors that, without destroying their own individuality, literary style, or personal interest, they produced His complete revelation to man. Although men did the actual writing, God inspired them. The Bible is God's message to man. It does not merely contain the Word of God; it *is* the Word of God.

Of course, God used various ways of getting His inspiration across. But regardless of whether God dictated the exact words, as He sometimes did, or whether the authors were led by God to copy ancient literature, which they themselves tell us they did, or their writings were the results of research, as the case of Luke, in every particular way, God guided men so that they wrote exactly what He intended for them to write. The result was that the Bible is the Word of God.

B. THEORIES OF INSPIRATION

There are various theories of inspiration, which we will now consider.

1. Key Issue: Dual Authorship

In trying to determine what is and what is not the true theory of inspiration, we need to consider the key issue with which people have been wrestling, which is dual authorship: the fact that the Bible was written both by God and by man. For example, Exodus 20:12 contains one of the Ten Commandments, which says: *Honor your father and your mother, that your days may be long in the land which Jehovah your God gives you.* According to Matthew 15:4, it was God who made that statement, but according to Mark 7:10, it was Moses. Is this contradictory? Not in the least, for it was God who was the ultimate author and Moses who was the means. This is an example of dual authorship. So Matthew can say that God said it, and Mark can say that Moses said it, and both are true.

Another example is the prophecy of Psalm 110:1, which reads: *The Lord said unto my Lord, Sit you at my right hand, Until I make your enemies your footstool.* Mark 12:36 tells us that the Holy Spirit made that statement, but in the very next verse (12:37), it is said that David made that statement. Both are true; David did the writing, but the Holy Spirit inspired him to do it. Again we have dual authorship.

A third example is in Exodus 3:6 and 15, where we have the statement: *I am the God of Abraham, the God of Isaac, and the God of Jacob.* Matthew 22:31-32 tells us it was God who made that statement, but Mark 12:26 and Luke 20:37 tell us that Moses did; and both are true.

A fourth example is Isaiah 6:9-10, where these verses prophesy the blinding of Israel. When John quotes these verses in John 12:39-41, he tells us that Isaiah made that statement, but when the same verses are quoted in Acts 28:25-27, Luke tells us that the Holy Spirit is the One who said these words. Again, both are true because the Bible has dual authorship.

Furthermore, we are sometimes told about both authors in the same passage. Psalm 69:25, for example, is quoted in Acts 1:16-20, where both David and the Holy Spirit are credited with saying these words. Psalm 2:1-2 are quoted in Acts 4:25-26, and again, both David and the Holy Spirit are given the credit. Isaiah 7:14 is quoted in Matthew 1:22-23, and both God and Isaiah the prophet are given the credit. Hosea 11:1 is quoted by Matthew 2:15, and both God and the prophet are given the credit.

Sometimes both authors are credited with the writing of a passage, which emphasizes the concept of dual authorship. The relationship of the two authors is that God is the primary and ultimate source, and man is the instrument God used. He is the ultimate cause, while man is the means.

This concept of dual authorship has given rise to four suggested solutions to the relationship between God and man. One solution is that the Bible is exclusively divine, but as we have seen, that is not what the Bible itself teaches. A second solution goes to the other extreme and teaches that the Bible is exclusively human, which again is contrary to clear statements in the Scriptures. A third suggested solution is that it is part divine and part human. This implies that God is only responsible for certain parts of the Bible, while other parts are exclusively human. This too, however, is not taught in Scripture.

The fourth solution is the best in trying to show the relationship between the divine Author and the human author. In this view, the Bible is a product of both the divine and the human without one being impaired by the other, and both are wholly present in every word from beginning to end. It is not that the Bible is totally divinely authored, nor is it completely the work of men. Instead, it should be understood that both God and man are totally responsible for every word, so that every word of Scripture is a product of both God and man. Hence we have this key idea that the Bible is a product of dual authorship. Unfortunately, this has produced a number of false theories regarding inspiration.[25]

2. False Theories

Altogether there are eight false theories of inspiration.

a. Natural or Intuition Theory

This false theory states that the Bible was written by men who possessed unusual religious insight; men who had superior insight on the part of natural man into moral and religious truth. The authors of Scripture simply had a higher development of natural insight. This theory says that the writers of Scripture were indeed inspired, but in the same way artists, poets, and musicians are inspired. Just as artists, poets, and musicians have produced masterpieces in art, poetry, and music, the writers of the Scriptures, having a higher level of inspiration, simply produced "masterpieces" in the area of religious thought.

The trouble with the theory of natural inspiration is that there is an overemphasis on the human side. In this theory, natural inspiration means only pure genius; there is nothing supernatural about it. Actually, it leads to self-contradiction, because, in this theory, one inspired writing can contradict another. That makes all the religious and spiritual thoughts of Scripture purely subjective. The natural inspiration or natural intuition theory does not adequately deal with the nature of the Bible.

b. Mystical or Illumination Theory

Basically, this theory is the same as the natural inspiration or natural intuition theory. The only difference between the two is that the first theory applies the concept of higher inspiration to all men in general, whereas this one limits it to believers and gives a bit more credit to the Holy Spirit. This theory allows for an intensification of religious perception on the part of some believers. This theory says that there was an intensification of the illumination of the Holy Spirit for some, and these are the ones who wrote the Scriptures. They go on to say that this is still possible today and believers, at any time, could write divine Scripture by divine energy.

---

[25] Question 1 on page 67

The problem with this theory is the same as the previous one; there is an overemphasis on the human authorship of Scripture, and it allows for more Scripture to be written today. Biblically speaking, illumination does not reveal new truth; it only helps in comprehending truth which has already been revealed. In this theory, inspiration is the work of the Holy Spirit but only in a higher degree of inner illumination. Furthermore, this theory does not believe that the writers were free from error. So the second theory does not really adequately deal with the high view of inspiration that the Bible demands for itself.

c. Partial Inspiration Theory

This false theory means exactly what it says: The Bible was inspired only in certain areas of doctrine, such as, precepts, and spiritual truths, knowable to the human authors. But it was not necessarily inspired in other areas such as, science, biology, geology, geography, or archaeology. It goes on to say that the Bible does contain inspiration, but it is not without error.

The problem with this theory is that it separates dual authorship too far apart, and it leads to a clear subjectivity by the reader, who then decides what is inspired and what is not inspired.

d. Degrees Inspiration Theory

This false theory is a little bit different than the partial inspiration theory. The degrees inspiration theory says that the whole Bible is inspired, not just parts of it, but also says not every part has been inspired to the same degree. This concept is reflected in the red-letter editions of the Scriptures, where the words of *Yeshua* are printed in red. Some believers have actually taken this to mean that it implies that the words of *Yeshua* were more inspired than the rest of the Scriptures, but He did not write them down; they were written by Matthew, Mark, Luke, and John.

The problem with this theory is that it claims that some parts of the Scriptures are more inspired than others. There is always some inspiration, but at the same time, this theory allows for lesser and greater degrees of error. The problem with this theory, like the previous one, is that it allows too much separation between the human and the divine. Like the previous theory, it leads to both speculation and subjectivity.

e. Conceptual Inspiration Theory

This false theory claims that only the thoughts of the Bible are inspired, but not the words. It teaches that God simply implanted ideas into the authors' minds, and these ideas were indeed inspired, but the authors were left completely to themselves to express these ideas in their own words.

This theory also allows too much separation between the human and the divine. It should always be remembered that ideas have to be expressed in terms of words. Ideas are not transferable except in words. This is not a good theory either.

f. Dynamic Inspiration Theory

This false theory means that the Bible is inspired only in those areas that concern the faith and life of a believer. There is an inerrancy in matters of faith and practice, inerrancy in the areas of spiritual truth and salvation. But it goes on to say that the Bible could have error in areas not related to faith and salvation. They believe in plenary inspiration, but they do not believe in verbal inspiration.

The problem with this theory is that it leads to both speculation and subjectivity. Who is going to decide what things are essential to faith and what things are not essential to faith? If the Bible cannot guarantee inerrancy in other parts of the Scriptures, there is no way it can guarantee inerrancy in the areas of faith and practice as well.

g. Mechanical or Dictation Inspiration Theory

This false theory teaches that the whole Bible was dictated word-for-word, from Genesis to Revelation, and thus the writers of Scripture were merely stenographers. The problem with this theory is that there is an overemphasis on the divine side of the authorship. If this theory were true, every part of the Bible would read exactly the same and have the same style. Yet, the writing styles are very different, making it clear that every book reflects the nuances of the writing style of the particular author God is using. Furthermore, in a dictation style, you would not find the personal comments and feelings of the human author inserted. Yet, in the Book of Jeremiah, he frequently describes his own personal feelings, which sometimes actually go contrary to what God expected of him as His prophet. Further, in Romans 9:1-3, Paul expresses his own personal concern. In a purely mechanical dictation, we would not see such personal expressions of feeling. The fact that the Bible's authors often express their own struggles and feelings shows that the dictation theory is false. There is no question that parts of Scripture, like the Ten Commandments, were dictated, but the dictated parts are only a very small portion of the Bible as a whole.

h. Neo-Orthodox Theory

This false theory teaches that the Bible is inspired because it becomes the Word of God. The Bible itself is not the Word of God, but it does contain the Word of God (the Word is Messiah and the Bible bears witness to the Word). Because it could become the Word of God in our lives, the Bible is inspired only in that way. So in neo-orthodoxy, the Bible contains the Word of God, but it is not directly the Word of God. Rather, God influenced the writers to record His great acts and their encounters with Him through these events. He now uses their writings to speak to the readers, and when an "encounter" happens between God and man, as he studies the Scriptures, it becomes God's Word. It is therefore only as a person reads and studies the Bible and has an encounter with God, it becomes the Word of God to that individual at that moment and point in time.

This view, like the other false theories, has some major problems. First, it is extremely subjective. Neo-orthodoxy writers are in total disagreement among themselves as to what does and what does not constitute the "encounter," and what is and is not inspired. They all talk about having had an encounter, and yet each encounter brings them to different conclusions! So since none of the actual statements of Scripture can be confidently equated with the Word of God, and it is denied that the Scriptures contain the actual statements of God, there is no way of knowing exactly what God is saying. As a result, the subjectivity of this theory leads to every man doing that which is right in his own eyes.

These are the eight false views of the theory of inspiration, and it brings us on to the next division, which gives us the true position: plenary verbal inspiration.[26]

3. The True Position: Plenary Verbal Inspiration

The only valid way of seeing how inspiration occurred is by the true theory, which is called the Plenary Verbal Inspiration Theory.

a. The Position

Plenary verbal inspiration means that the Bible is completely inspired; it is at the same time the Word of God and the words of human authors. God is the source, but He used humans to write the words.

---

[26] Question 2 on page 67

Plenary inspiration means that the inspiration of Scripture extends to every portion of the Scriptures. The word "plenary" means "full and complete." The Bible is the final authority not only in matters of faith and practice, but it is authoritative on any subject to which the Bible addresses itself. Anything the Bible affirms to be true is true. It is not only true in matters of faith and practice, but it is true on every issue to which it speaks. If it says something about science, it can be trusted. If it says something about geology, it can be trusted. If it says something about archaeology, it can be trusted. If it says something about sociology, it can be trusted. Every subject to which the Bible speaks and which it affirms as true is true. Plenary inspiration is fully complete; it extends to every portion of the Scriptures; it is the final authority as to truth on all the subjects it addresses.

Verbal inspiration emphasizes the words themselves in that the Holy Spirit guided the words to be chosen and used. God respected the human authors to the extent that each writer's style and characteristics were preserved. Out of the author's vocabulary, it was God who chose the words that would be written down. The words that were chosen by the author were the very words that God wanted them to use. Verbal inspiration means that inspiration extended to the very words written by the writers. This does not mean dictation. The whole Bible was not dictated word-for-word; only parts of it were. Verbal inspiration simply means that God allowed the authors to use their own characteristics, style, and vocabulary. When they chose from the vocabulary they normally used, it was God who actually directed them in the choosing of those words.

Another important word to include in dealing with the true theory of inspiration is the word infallible. Infallibility means "unfailing accuracy." The Bible is unfailingly accurate in every topic to which it speaks; this makes the Bible trustworthy. Another key word is inerrant. There is no false statement or fact in the original writings; this makes the Bible truthful. Plenary verbal inspiration means that the Bible is fully inspired in every part, down to the very words chosen. It is infallible with unfailing accuracy and therefore trustworthy; it is inerrant in that it contains no false statement, no error, and is therefore truthful.

(1) Five Things Plenary Verbal Inspiration Did not Accomplish

First, it did not overwhelm the author's personality. The personalities of the forty individual writers manifest themselves through their writings. One gets a different concept of Peter from what he wrote, as compared to Paul and what he wrote.

Second, plenary verbal inspiration did not render the author's intelligence void of use. The author's intelligence was used by God to produce these writings.

The third thing it did not do was to exempt them from personal research. For example, Luke 1:1-4 states that he carefully researched other writings and narrations before he sat down to write his own biography of the life of Messiah. Even other writers, such as the author of the Book of Judges, mentioned other books that they resorted to in doing their research. While it did not exempt personal research, inspiration is seen in that God so directed these authors to other writings that, when they chose statements from those other writings, they chose only those statements that were true and only those statements which God wanted them to choose. God so directed them that they never chose a statement that was false.

The fourth thing that plenary verbal inspiration did not do is to prohibit the use of other materials. For instance, when Luke chose to write his gospel, we know he used other sources, which perhaps included the Gospels of Matthew and Mark.

The fifth thing that plenary verbal inspiration did not do is it did not mean that the author always understood what he wrote. A good example of this is Daniel. Several times Daniel stated that, when he finished writing, he did not understand what he wrote. He knew that he used the words God wanted him to use, but he confessed that he did not clearly understand what he was writing. Verbal inspiration did not mean that the author always understood what he wrote, for quite often he did not.

(2) Five Things Plenary Verbal Inspiration Did Accomplish

First, it preserved the original authors from error. When the original writings were finally produced by each of the forty writers of Scripture, there was not a single mistake, not a single error, contained in any of the sixty-six books.

The second thing verbal inspiration did was to preserve the Scriptures from omissions. None of the authors left out anything God wanted them to include. Everything God wanted them to include was included.

The third thing it did was to preserve the authors from making inclusions of things God did not want in the Scriptures. For example, there might have been other true things—they may be very true—but God did not desire to have them included in His Word. So plenary verbal inspiration means that they were preserved from including what God did not want them to include. That is the other side of the coin: On one hand, they did not omit what God wanted included; on the other hand, they did not include that which God wanted omitted.

The fourth thing plenary verbal inspiration did was that it assured appropriate wording. God allowed the human authors to use their own style and vocabulary, but the words they chose out of their own vocabulary were the very words God wanted them to put down and in the very order that He wanted the words put down. Both Greek and Hebrew allow for different word orders, but God superintended in such a way that they had appropriate wordings; the authors wrote the very words in the order God wanted them written.

The fifth thing that plenary verbal inspiration did was that it meant a co-authorship of the divine and the human. Both God and man produced the Scriptures, but God was the source while man was the means or the instrument. Therefore, no part of Scripture is produced solely as the work of man; every word was superintended, directed by God.

It should also be understood that plenary verbal inspiration does not mean that every single statement in the Bible is true, because the Bible does actually record the lies and false statements made by fallen angels and unbelieving men. For example, it records a false statement made by Satan about the character of Job. Obviously, the statement made by Satan is not true. In this case, inspiration simply guarantees that Satan really did make that statement; that it was a true event. Inspiration does not mean that Satan's lie was true, but that it is a fact that he really did say it. Inspiration guarantees that everything the Bible affirms to be true, is true, in every area of knowledge upon which it touches. This includes the lies and false statements of certain men and angels, and it guarantees that such statements really were made. Therefore we can believe the biblical record in all these areas.[27]

b. Evidence for Plenary Verbal Inspiration

(1) Key Passages

There are three key Scriptures relating to plenary verbal inspiration. The first one is found in II Timothy 3:16-17:

> [16] *Every scripture inspired of God is also profitable for teaching, for reproof, for correction, for instruction which is in righteousness:* [17] *that the man of God may be complete, furnished completely unto every good work.*

The main emphasis in this passage is on plenary inspiration. It states, *Every Scripture*, or all Scripture, is inspired. The Greek word for Scripture here is the word

---

[27] Question 3 on page 67

γραφὴ (*graphe*) which, as we saw in Chapter 2, has to do with written revelation. The words πᾶσα γραφὴ ("All Scripture") refer to "all" written revelation.

The second emphasis in this verse on plenary inspiration is that it is given by inspiration of God. The Greek word translated *inspired of God* is θεόπνευστος (*theopneustos*), literally meaning "God-breathed," thus the Scriptures are the "out-breathing" of God. So, technically, we are not so much talking about in-spiring but about out-spiring. The Scriptures are the very things that God has out-breathed or inspired.

The third thing to note in this passage is the result of this out-breathing of God, which is profitable in four areas: in *teaching*, in *reproof*, in *correction*, and in *instruction ... in righteousness*. This does not mean, of course, that every verse is profitable in all four of these areas. However, it does mean that every verse of Scripture will be profitable in one or more of these areas.

The second key passage relating to plenary verbal inspiration is II Peter 1:21: *For no prophecy ever came by the will of man; but men spoke from God being moved by the Holy Spirit*. The emphasis of this passage is on the means of inspiration. This particular verse makes three points. First, *no prophecy ever came by the will of man*. In other words, the primary source of revelation was always God, while man was always merely the secondary source or the means of writing Scripture. Second, the passage says that *men spoke from God*, so that when the prophets spoke, they spoke the Word of God. But once again, they were only the secondary source. The words they spoke were God's words, meaning the will of the writers did not direct the writing of the text. Third, they spoke as they were *being moved by the Holy Spirit*. The Greek word translated as "being moved" (φέρω) means "to carry along," or "bear along." In Acts 27:15 and 17, it is used of a ship being borne along, driven, directed, and carried about by the wind, yet the sailors were still active. It is the same word found in Acts 27:15, 17 that speaks of a ship at sea being "borne along" or being carried along by water. The picture here is that the prophets were borne along by the Holy Spirit as they wrote, and men transcribed what was out-breathed. These men were transcribing as they were being borne along, moved along, and carried along by the Holy Spirit.

The third passage relating to plenary verbal inspiration is found in I Corinthians 2:13: *Which things also we speak, not in words which man's wisdom teaches, but which the Spirit teaches; combining spiritual things with spiritual words*. This passage puts emphasis on the words themselves being inspired. It was the Holy Spirit who brought God's thoughts to the writers, yet not just were their thoughts inspired, but also their very words. This required inerrancy.

(2) Other Lines of Evidence

Having looked at the key passages that clearly spell out the fact that the Bible was plenarily and verbally inspired, what other evidences support this theory? We will be discussing six points.

i. God's character

The very character of God requires that the Scriptures He produces be plenary and verbally inspired. If God revealed Himself in written form, would it not be an accurate revelation? The implication of Romans 3:4 is that by virtue of His character, that which God produces must reflect the same character. Therefore, if the Scriptures are the out-breathing of God, then indeed, they must be the inspired Word of God.

ii. Old Testament Claims

Clearly, plenary, verbal inspiration is what the Old Testament claims for itself. We see this in seven ways:

1) A total of 3,808 times it says, *Thus saith Jehovah,* or *Jehovah said,* or *the Word of the* LORD *(or Jehovah) came.*
2) There are specific commands to record the words of the Lord. Moses received such commands in Exodus 17:14; 24:3-4; 34:27; Numbers 33:2; and Deuteronomy 31:9, 24-25. Jeremiah was told this in 30:2; 36:1-4, 28; and 32. Daniel was told to write the words of God in 12:4.
3) God authenticated the five books of Moses elsewhere in the Old Testament (Josh. 1:7-8; Num. 8:1; Is. 8:20; Mal. 4:4; Ps. 19:7). The whole of Psalm 119 keeps referring back to the authority of the Law of Moses as being the Word of God.
4) There is the authentication of the prophetic books in passages like II Chronicles 36:15-16; II Kings 17:13; Zechariah 7:7, 12; and 8:9. These references will be found to authenticate previous prophets.
5) Isaiah's book itself is called "The Book of Jehovah," in Isaiah 34:16.
6) God authenticated Jeremiah's book, in Jeremiah 25:13.
7) Some Old Testament writers quote Old Testament writers with authority. For instance, Joshua 8:30-35 speaks for the Law of Moses. Joel 2:32 quotes Obadiah 17. Micah 4:1-4 quotes Isaiah 2:2-4. Jeremiah 26:17-19

quotes Micah 3:12. Daniel 9:1-3 and Ezra 1:1-4 both are based upon Jeremiah 25:11-12 and 29:10.

iii. New Testament as Witness to the Old Testament

The New Testament contains three hundred quotations from the Old Testament; seventy of these came from the Law of Moses, one hundred seventy came from the Prophets, and sixty came from the Writings. Various quotes state that God was the speaker, such as in Matthew 15:4 and Acts 28:25. Of course, II Timothy 3:16-17 and II Peter 1:21 clearly have the Old Testament in mind. Besides three hundred direct quotations from the Old Testament, there are also 4,105 allusions to the Old Testament. The New Testament claims a total of fifty-six times that God was the author of the Old Testament.

iv. The Messiah as Witness

Messiah's own witness to the Old Testament is a fourth evidence for plenary verbal inspiration. *Yeshua* Himself accepted the Old Testament as being the inspired Word of God. This we can show in five ways.

First, *Yeshua* accepted the Old Testament in its entirety and made many references to the historical accounts. Luke 24:44 points out that He accepted all three divisions of the Old Testament: The Law, the Prophets, and the Writings. He also made allusions to specific individuals in the Old Testament, such as Adam and Eve (Mat. 19:4-6), Abel (Mat. 23:35), Noah (Mat. 24:37), Sodom (Lk. 17:29), Abraham (Jn. 8:56), Moses (Mk. 12:26), David (Mat. 12:3), Solomon (Mat. 12:42), Elijah (Lk. 4:25), Jonah (Mat. 12:39-41), Isaiah (Mat. 12:7), Daniel (Mat. 24:15), Abiathar (Mk. 2:26), and the Patriarchs (Mat. 8:11). These references to historical accounts in the Hebrew Scriptures are compelling evidence that *Yeshua* accepted the Old Testament in its entirety as being the inspired Word of God.

Second, in Matthew 5:17, when speaking of the Law of Moses, *Yeshua* said He had not come to destroy the law but to fulfill it. The reason He came to fulfill the law is because He accepted it as being the inspired Word of God.

Third, in John 10:35, *Yeshua* said, *The Scripture cannot be broken*. He was speaking of Psalm 82:6, which is a section from the Writings, and He would not have made such a statement if He did not consider the Old Testament to be the inspired Word of God.

Fourth, in Matthew 23:35, He makes the inclusive statement, *from Abel to Zechariah*. Abel is found in the Book of Genesis, which is the first book in the Jewish order of the Old Testament. Zechariah is found in the Book of II Chronicles, which is the last book in the Jewish order. *Yeshua* clearly accepted everything from Genesis to II Chronicles or, as we would say, "from Genesis to Revelation."

A fifth way of illustrating Messiah's witness to the Old Testament as being the inspired Word of God is in the way He used it with authority. He used it as the basis of His teaching. In Matthew 4:17, He taught about the Kingdom based upon Daniel 2:44. His teaching on divorce in Matthew 19:4-6 was based upon the Book of Deuteronomy, and the greatest commandment found in Matthew 22:37 was quoted from Deuteronomy 6:4-5. Thus, Yeshua used the Old Testament as the basis for His teaching.

Yeshua also used the Old Testament as the explanation of His own Person. He authenticated His message and His claims by referring to the Old Testament. In Luke 4:18, He quoted Isaiah 61:1-2 and referred it to Himself. In Matthew 11:1-6, He quoted Isaiah 35:5-6 and referred it to Himself.

Additionally, *Yeshua* always made the Old Testament the final appeal in any debate. By quoting the Old Testament, He was basically stating that it was the end of the argument. Examples of this are Matthew 12:5-7, 22, and 29. So the fourth evidence for plenary verbal inspiration is Messiah's own witness to the Old Testament.

v. Pre-Authentication of the Messiah

The New Testament contains a witness to itself as a fifth evidence for plenary verbal inspiration.

1) *Yeshua* Himself pre-authenticated the New Testament writings in John 14:26 and 16:12-14. He did this by pointing out that the Holy Spirit would *bring to remembrance* among His disciples everything that He had taught them, so that when the time came, they would be able to put it into writing.

2) When Peter was writing, he was conscious that he was writing the very Word of God (I Peter 1:11-12).

3) Paul too was conscious that he was writing the Word of God and says so in I Corinthians 2:13; 14:37; II Corinthians 13:3; Galatians 1:11-12; I Thessalonians 2:13; 4:2, 8; Ephesians 3:3-4, 8; Titus 1:2-3.

4) Peter authenticates the writings of Paul, even calling them "Scripture" (II Peter 3:15-16).

5) Several times, John the Apostle was specifically commanded to write down the revelation he was receiving from God (Rev. 1:11 and 19; 21:5; 22:16, 18, and 19).

6) Peter equated the words of the apostles with those of the prophets (II Peter 3:2).

7) One part of the New Testament quotes another part of the New Testament as being authoritative. For example, Jude 18-19 quotes II Peter 3:2-3. First Timothy 5:18 quotes both Deuteronomy 25:4, from the Old Testament, and Luke 10:7, from the New Testament, and sees them as having equal authority. Finally, I Corinthians 11:24-26 quotes Luke 22:17-20.

vi. Verbal Inspiration

Both the Old and New Testaments affirm verbal inspiration, not just plenary inspiration. In the Old Testament, we see this in Exodus 4:10-15; 20:1; Deuteronomy 4:2; 18:18-19; II Samuel 23:2; Isaiah 59:21; and Jeremiah 1:7-9. These passages clearly confirm the verbal inspiration; the emphasis is on the words of Scripture.

The New Testament also affirms verbal inspiration in at least seven ways.

1) In Matthew 22:43-45, Messiah based his argument upon one single word: "Lord." If the Scriptures were not verbally inspired, then it would be foolish to rest a case purely upon one word, and yet, that is exactly what *Yeshua* did.

2) In John 6:63, there is an emphasis on words.

3) In John 10:34-36, there is an argument based upon the word "gods."

4) In John 17:8, the words of the apostles are the words of Messiah and the words of the Father.

5) In Galatians 3:16, the argument is based upon the singular word "seed." This example is crucial insofar as the argument is not only based upon a word, but upon the fact that this word is in the singular and not in the plural. Paul's argument rests upon the singularity of the word "seed," which he applies to Messiah.

6) In Matthew 4:4, *Yeshua* quoted Deuteronomy and said that man lives by every word that proceeds out of the mouth of God.

7) In Matthew 5:17-18, He put emphasis on the very letters of Scripture when He said that *not the smallest letter or stroke shall pass from the Law until all is accomplished.*

These passages show that the New Testament teaches verbal inspiration. Many of the arguments made by *Yeshua* and the authors of the New Testament were based upon a single word of the Old Testament. If verbal inspiration were not true, then the New Testament writers would be proved faulty in establishing their arguments upon this.

vii. Inerrancy

There are a number of passages which clearly emphasize the inerrancy of Scripture and maintain that the Bible is free from error. Some of these passages are Psalm 19:7-9; 111:7; 119:160; Proverbs 30:5; Luke 1:4; John 10:35; 19:35; II Timothy 3:16; and Titus 1:2.

d. Objections to Plenary Verbal Inspiration

Moving on to the fourth part of our study on plenary verbal inspiration, we have to consider the main objections to it. The critics and the unbelievers in the inspiration of Scripture have raised a number of objections to the whole doctrine of plenary verbal inspiration, and these objections can be divided into four main areas.

(1) Science and History

Some scientists say that the Scriptures contradict theories that are known to be true by scientists. Some historians say that the Bible contains historical errors. The answer is simple. First, while the Bible does contradict certain scientific theories, it has never yet contradicted a scientific fact. Second, where relevant historical documents exist, they have shown the Bible to be absolutely accurate.

It should be remembered that the Bible does use phenomenological language (the language of appearance). The Bible speaks about the sun "rising" and "setting." Of course, everyone knows that the sun does not "rise" and "set." In actuality, it only appears to rise and set. In reality, the earth is turning on its axis. That is the language of appearance, and even scientists, who know better, speak about sunrises and sunsets. When the Bible uses the language of appearance, it is not saying that the sun really does rise and really does set, but that that is the way it appears. Scientists use this same language of appearance and should not resort to a double standard when critiquing the Scriptures.

The Bible is not a textbook on science or history. But again, whenever it touches on science and whenever it touches on history, it has been shown to be absolutely accurate. Nothing in geology or anthropology has shown the Bible to be inaccurate. The field of archaeology has shown the Bible to be historically accurate; physical laws have shown the Bible to be scientifically accurate; and historical geography has shown the Bible to be geographically accurate. The objections coming from science and history have yet to provide clear evidence that the Bible contains one point of error.

(2) Skepticism of Prophecy and Miracles

This objection presupposes that the supernatural does not exist. But if there were a God, and therefore all that the concept of God implies, then miracles and predictive prophecy are not problems. If God exists, then the supernatural exists. If what we mean by "God" really is, miracles can exist and predictive prophecy can exist. In fact, fulfilled prophecy has proven the accuracy of the Scripture. Fulfilled prophecy is the evidence that unfulfilled prophecy will be fulfilled in the future.

(3) Morals and Religions

The objector likes to point out how terrible some of the heroes of the Bible were. They point out such things as David's adultery with Bathsheba and his murder of Uriah or Noah's drunkenness. The fact that the Bible records the immorality and the lack of spirituality on the part of its biblical heroes shows that the Bible is accurate. There are other religious books that only emphasize the heroics of their leaders, but the Bible emphasizes both the strong and the weak points.

For example, the various sinful acts of biblical heroes are recorded, but they are not sanctioned. Noah's drunkenness in Genesis 9 is recorded, but it is not sanctioned. Lot's incest in Genesis 19 is recorded, but not sanctioned. Jacob's lie in Genesis 27 is recorded, but not sanctioned. David's adultery in II Samuel 11 is recorded, but not sanctioned. Solomon's polygamy in I Kings 11 is recorded, but not sanctioned. The Bible does record the sinful acts of its human heroes, but to record these sinful acts does not mean to sanction them.

Furthermore, sometimes wrongful acts, immoral or sinful acts, may appear to be sanctioned, but it is the faith and the intent that is sanctioned, not the act itself. For example, when Rahab lied to her own king, it was not Rahab's duplicity that was sanctioned, but Rahab's faith (Heb. 11:31; Jas. 2:25); it is Jael's faith and not her treachery that was sanctioned (Judg. 4—5); it was Samson's actions, not his lusts, which were sanctioned (Judg. 14—16; Heb. 11:32).

Sometimes, people point out the fact that certain heroes of Scripture clearly contradict a command of the Lord, and yet they are not taken to task for it. Sometimes, this is because of the difference of dispensations. Not every commandment applies to every dispensation. For example, God told Noah that he could eat anything that moved, but God told Moses that he could eat only certain things. Now, through Paul, God declared that man might again eat anything with thanksgiving. One should be careful not to assume that a command has been broken, because not every command applies to every dispensation.

These objections, which come out of the areas of morals and religions, are often a subjective judgment or simply a misunderstanding of what the Bible actually sanctions and what it does not sanction.

(4) New Testament Quotations of the Old Testament

A fourth major area of objections comes from the area of New Testament quotations of the Old Testament. In looking at the context, such Old Testament passages can seem to not really be saying what the New Testament writer is trying to make it say. This causes some to doubt verbal inspiration. We need to recognize that the New Testament quotes the Old Testament in four different ways, and a proper understanding of these ways will eliminate this objection.

When the rabbis quoted the Hebrew Bible, they would do it in one of four different categories. The acronym they used was *PaRDeS*. The four capital letters stand for the four categories while the small letters are inserting the vowel points. The "P" stands for *Pshat* which means "simple." This is viewed as the natural meaning of the text, and the actual prophecies are understood that way. This would fall under the category of "Literal Prophecy plus Literal Fulfillment." The "R" stands for *Remez* which means "hint." This would fall under the category of "Literal plus Typical." It does not deny the literal meaning of the text but shows that the person or event or thing is a type of something else. The letter "D" stands for *Drash* which means "explanation" or "exposition." This falls into the category of "Literal plus Application." Based upon one small point of similarity, the verse is applied to a current situation of the writer quoting the passage. It does not deny the original context, be it historic or prophetic, but because of one point of similarity, the verse is applied to a similar, but not exact situation. The "S" stands for *Sod* which means "secret" or "hidden." This falls into the category of "Summation" where the writer is not quoting any specific passage but summarizes what the Scriptures teach about a specific person or situation or future event.

The New Testament writers were Jews who followed the same four categories. However, they did not do what is often practiced in covenant theology or replacement theology. The theologians adhering to these doctrines claim that what the Hebrew Bible states about God's blessings for Israel will not be fulfilled in, by, or through Israel but in, by, or through the Church and that therefore the Church is the "True Israel." But that was not the intent of the New Testament writers. Like the rabbis, they did not deny what was intended in the original text. They are simply showing typologies or making applications without denying the original meaning. The following are specific examples from the New Testament.

i. Literal Prophecy plus Literal Fulfillment – *Pshat*

The first category is known as "literal prophecy plus literal fulfillment." The example of this first category is found in Matthew 2:5–6:

> ⁵ *And they said unto him, In Bethlehem of Judaea: for thus it is written through the prophet,* ⁶ *And Bethlehem, land of Judah, are in no wise least among the princes of Judah: For out of you shall come forth a governor, who shall be shepherd of my people Israel.*

This passage in the New Testament quotes Micah 5:2. If we go back to the context of Micah 5:2 to see what the Old Testament was talking about, we discover that it is dealing with the birth of the Messiah. The point of Micah 5:2 is that when the Messiah is born, He will be born in the town of Bethlehem in the region of Judah and nowhere else; not the Bethlehem of Galilee, and not any other town in Judah. That is the *literal* meaning, the *literal* interpretation of Micah 5:2; the Messiah, when He is born, will be born in the town of Bethlehem, within the tribal territory of Judah.

In the New Testament, there is a literal fulfillment of that literal prophecy. *Yeshua*, when He was born as the Messiah, was born in the town of Bethlehem, and no other town in the tribal region of Judah. Furthermore, He was born in Bethlehem of Judah and not Bethlehem of Galilee. This was a *literal* fulfillment of Micah 5:2, by which the New Testament quotes the Old Testament—*literal prophecy plus literal fulfillment*. The prophecy makes only one point. When it is fulfilled in the New Testament in a perfect way, the New Testament quotes the Old Testament.

Another example of this first category is Matthew 1:22–23:

> ²² *Now all this is come to pass, that it might be fulfilled which was spoken by the Lord through the prophet, saying,* ²³ *Behold, the virgin shall be with child, and shall bring forth a son, And they shall call his name Immanuel; which is, being interpreted, God with us.*

This is a quotation of Isaiah 7:14. The context of Isaiah 7:14 is predicting that when the Messiah is born, He will be born of a virgin. That is the *literal* meaning of Isaiah 7:14. In the New Testament, there is a *literal* fulfillment of the *literal* prophecy, and so the passage is quoted by the New Testament.

Yet another example is found in Matthew 3:3, which quotes Isaiah 40:3, and in Mark 1:2, which quotes Malachi 3:1. Both the Isaiah and Malachi passages predict that before the Messiah is made known, He will be preceded by a forerunner. A forerunner will announce the soon coming of the King. This *literal* prophecy was fulfilled in a *literal* way by John the Baptist, and for that reason, the verses in Isaiah and Malachi were quoted by Matthew, Mark, and Luke.

Then there is Luke 4:18–19, which quotes Isaiah 61:1–2. The context in the Isaiah account is speaking of the kind of ministry the Messiah was to have at His First Coming, the nature and style of His ministry. In Luke, *Yeshua* was *literally* fulfilling that prophecy, so it is quoted.

So is Matthew 4:13–16, which quotes Isaiah 8:22–9:2. The context of that prophecy is speaking of the ministry of the Messiah, whose major area of ministry will be within the tribal territories of Zebulun and Naphtali, which is the *literal* prophecy of Isaiah 9:1–2. In the New Testament, *Yeshua* ministered primarily in these two tribal territories. Nazareth was within the tribal territory of Zebulun, and Capernaum was within the tribal territory of Naphtali. He grew up in the tribal territory of Zebulun and headquartered his ministry in the tribal territory of Naphtali. In this way, the prophecy was *literally* fulfilled.

Another example of this first category is Matthew 21:5, which quotes Zechariah 9:9. The context of Zechariah 9:9 speaks about the Messiah riding into Jerusalem upon a donkey. When *Yeshua*, in His triumphal entry, rode into Jerusalem on that type of an animal, then that prophecy was *literally* fulfilled. Therefore, it is quoted by the New Testament.

Then there is John 12:38, which quotes Isaiah 53:1. Isaiah 53:1 clearly prophesies that when the Messiah comes, He is going to be rejected by His own people. When *Yeshua* was rejected by Israel, that was a *literal* fulfillment of that particular prophecy. It is quoted again in the first category of a *literal* prophecy plus a *literal* fulfillment.

Also in this category of prophecy is John 19:24 which states:

They said therefore one to another, Let us not rend it, but cast lots for it, whose it shall be: that the scripture might be fulfilled, which says, They parted my garments among them, And upon my vesture did they cast lots.

John quotes Psalm 22:18, and the context of that verse speaks of the death of the Messiah. Part of the death scene is that His clothing will be taken away from Him and the tormentors will gamble for His clothes. That is the *literal* meaning of the prophecy of Psalm 22:18. In the New Testament, there is a *literal* fulfillment of this particular prophecy. When the Roman soldiers gambled for the clothing of *Yeshua*, they fulfilled the prophecy. For that reason, John quoted that prophecy in this particular passage.

Closely related is another quotation found in Matthew 27:46:

And about the ninth hour Yeshua cried with a loud voice, saying, Eli, Eli, lama sabachthani? that is My God, my God, why have you forsaken me?

Here, Matthew quoted Psalm 22:1. The context of Psalm 22:1 is speaking about the sufferings of the Messiah and the death of the Messiah. During His sufferings, He was to cry, *My God, my God, why have you forsaken me?* When *Yeshua* cried this, it was a direct fulfillment of the Old Testament prophecy, and for that reason, it was quoted in this New Testament passage.

This is the first category of New Testament quotations of the Old Testament: *literal prophecy plus literal fulfillment*. In these cases, the Old Testament *literally* speaks of a specific event in the future. When that specific event is *literally* fulfilled in the context of the New Testament, the New Testament quotes that particular prophecy as a point-by-point fulfillment. Many of the quotations of the Old Testament in the New Testament fall into this category.

ii. Literal plus Typical (Typology) – *Remez*

The second category of quotations can be labeled "literal plus typical." An example of this category is found in Matthew 2:15:

and was there until the death of Herod: that it might be fulfilled which was spoken by the Lord through the prophet, saying, Out of Egypt did I call my son.

If we go back to the context of Hosea 11:1, which is what this passage is quoting, we discover that it is not even a prophecy; it is speaking of a literal historical event, which was the Exodus. The background to Hosea 11:1 is Exodus 4:22–23. Israel, as a nation, is the son of God: *Israel is my son, my firstborn*. When God brought Israel out of Egypt, it is pictured by Hosea 11:1 as God bringing His son out of the land of Egypt. That is the *literal* meaning of Hosea 11:1. It is a historical verse dealing with a historical event, the Exodus. However, the literal Old Testament event becomes a *type* of a New Testament event. Now there is a more ideal Son of God, the individual Son of God, the Messianic Son of God, the Messiah Himself. When

Yeshua as a babe was brought out of the land of Egypt, God was again bringing His Son out of Egypt. This is a type and anti-type. The *type* was Israel, the national son, coming out of Egypt. The *anti-type* is the Messianic Son of God also coming out of Egypt. This is an example of the second category—*literal plus typical*.

Another example is Matthew 15:7–9:

[7] Ye hypocrites, well did Isaiah prophesy of you, saying, [8] This people honors me with their lips; But their heart is far from me. [9] But in vain do they worship me, Teaching (as their) doctrines the precepts of men.

Matthew 15:7–9 contains a quotation of Isaiah 29:13. The context of Isaiah 29:13 is speaking of a historical event when the people were rejecting the prophetic word of Isaiah the Prophet. The *literal* meaning of Isaiah 29:13 deals with Israel's rejection of the prophet. Israel's rejection of the prophetic word of the prophet becomes a *type* of Israel's rejection of the prophetic word of the Messiah, and so the Old Testament is quoted.

Also in this category is John 12:39–40:

[39] For this cause they could not believe, for that Isaiah said again, [40] He hath blinded their eyes, and he hardened their heart; Lest they should see with their eyes, and perceive with their heart, And should turn, And I should heal them.

Here, John quoted Isaiah 6:10, which in context states that the prophetic message of Isaiah the Prophet will be rejected by his own people. And that is the *literal* meaning of this passage. Again, Israel's rejection of the prophetic word of Isaiah the Prophet now becomes a *type* of the rejection of the prophetic word of the Messiah. For that reason, the Old Testament verse is quoted in this particular situation.

Yet another example in this category is found in Matthew 21:42:

Yeshua says unto them, Did ye never read in the scriptures, The stone which the builders rejected, The same was made the head of the corner; This was from the Lord, And it is marvelous in our eyes?

This passage quotes Psalm 118:22–23. In the context of that Psalm account, the point which is made is that a stone which the builders did not know what to do with was rejected or set aside. Later, when they finished the building, they realized that it was the top stone, the chief stone, that was the head of the corner. That is the *literal* meaning of Psalm 118:22–23. The rejection of the stone and the acceptance of the stone become a *type* of Israel's rejection and later acceptance of the Messiahship of *Yeshua*.

One more example of the second category is in John 19:36:

For these things came to pass, that the scripture might be fulfilled, A bone of him shall not be broken.

Here, John quoted Exodus 12:46. In the context of Exodus 12:46, Moses was dealing with a historical event that had to do with the Passover lamb that would save the Jews from the last plague. In the process of slaughtering the lamb, then roasting and eating it, the instruction was that not a bone of this Passover lamb was to be broken. That is the *literal* meaning of this command. The Passover lamb is a *type* of the Messiah, who is Messiah our Passover (I Cor. 5:7). During the process of His death by means of crucifixion, His bones were not broken while the bones of the other men crucified left and right of Him were broken. This was a fulfillment in a typical sense, not in a literal, prophetic sense.

This is in the second category—*literal plus typical*. The *literal* meaning deals with a historical event or thing and not a prophetic event. However, that historical event becomes a *type* of a New Testament event, and, therefore, it is quoted in that way. The Book of Hebrews uses this category frequently (the sin of Kadesh Barnea, the Tabernacle, the sacrificial system, the Aaronic priesthood, the Melchizedekian priesthood, etc.).

iii. Literal plus Application – *Drash*

The third category is "literal plus application." The example of this category is in Matthew 2:17–18:

[17] Then was fulfilled that which was spoken through Jeremiah the prophet, saying, [18] A voice was heard in Ramah, Weeping and great mourning, Rachel weeping for her children; And she would not be comforted, because they are not.

This time, Matthew quotes Jeremiah 31:15. In the original context, Jeremiah is speaking of a current event soon to come as the Babylonian Captivity begins. As the Jewish young men were being taken away into captivity, they went by the town of Ramah. Not too far from Ramah is where Rachel was buried, and she was the Old Testament symbol of Jewish motherhood. As the young Jewish men were marched toward Babylon, the Jewish mothers of Ramah came out weeping for the sons they would never see again. Jeremiah pictured this as "Rachel weeping for her children; And she would not be comforted, because they are not." Rachel weeping symbolized Jewish mothers weeping. That is the *literal* meaning of Jeremiah 31:15. In the New Testament, because of one simple point of similarity, that verse is

The Inspiration of the Scriptures

quoted. It is not a literal fulfillment, nor a full-scale typology, but simply an application because of one point of similarity. In the New Testament case, the one point of similarity was: Jewish mothers weeping for sons they will never see again, because Herod had slaughtered all the males of Bethlehem from the age of two years and under. Jewish mothers were again weeping for their sons. Everything else is different. In Jeremiah, the event takes place at Ramah, north of Jerusalem; in Matthew, it takes place in Bethlehem, south of Jerusalem. In Jeremiah the sons are still alive but are going into captivity; in Matthew the sons are dead. Because of one point of similarity, the New Testament quotes the Old Testament as an *application* only.

Another example of this same type of quotation is found in Acts 2:16–21:

> [16] *but this is that which has been spoken through the prophet Joel:* [17] *And it shall be in the last days, says God, I will pour forth of My Spirit upon all flesh: And your sons and your daughters shall prophesy, And your young men shall see visions, And your old men shall dream dreams:* [18] *Yea and on My servants and on My handmaidens in those days Will I pour forth of My Spirit; and they shall prophesy.* [19] *And I will show wonders in the heaven above, And signs on the earth beneath; Blood, and fire, and vapor of smoke:* [20] *The sun shall be turned into darkness. And the moon into blood, Before the day of the Lord come, That great and notable (day).* [21] *And it shall be, that whosoever shall call on the name of the Lord shall be saved.*

In this passage, Peter quoted Joel 2:28–32. The *literal* meaning of the Joel passage is in reference to the outpouring of the Holy Spirit upon the whole nation of Israel, resulting in supernatural manifestations. Nothing predicted by Joel 2 happened in Acts 2. For example, Joel spoke about the pouring out of the Spirit upon *all* Jewish flesh, which did not happen in the Book of Acts. In Acts 2, the Spirit was poured out upon twelve or, at the most, one hundred and twenty. Joel spoke about the sons and daughters of Israel prophesying, the young men seeing visions and the old men dreaming. None of that happened in Acts 2. No one did any prophesying, the young men did not see visions, and old men did not dream dreams. None of these are mentioned in the context of Acts 2. Furthermore, the servants of the Jewish people were to experience these same things, and there were no servants involved in the context of Acts 2. Joel spoke of climactic events in the heavens and on earth: blood, fire, pillars of smoke, with the sun turning into darkness, and the moon into blood, yet none of these things happened in Acts 2.

Nothing predicted by Joel Two happened in Acts 2, and what *did* happen in Acts 2 is not even mentioned in Joel 2. What did happen in Acts 2 was a manifestation of the Spirit, resulting in the speaking of tongues. Joel did not mention the gift of tongues at all. What we have here is the third category of quotation—*literal plus application*. The *literal* meaning of the Joel passage speaks of Israel's national salvation, when the Holy Spirit will be poured out on all Israel, resulting in Israel's national salvation in preparation for the Messianic Kingdom. Of course, that did not happen in the Book of Acts, but there was one point of similarity. That one point of similarity was an outpouring of the Holy Spirit, resulting in a unique manifestation, which, in that case, was the speaking in tongues. Because of one point of similarity—the outpouring of the Holy Spirit—the Old Testament was quoted by the New Testament as an *application*.

English idiomatic expressions do the same thing. For example, we sometimes say, "He met his Waterloo." What do we mean by that? We do not mean that the man went to Waterloo in Belgium and got defeated in a battle. The expression goes back to a historical event. That historical event had to do with Napoleon, whose imperial ambitions finally collapsed with his defeat at the Battle of Waterloo. Because of one point of similarity, defeat of an ambition, we often use that expression of someone whose ambitions are suddenly destroyed by some climactic event in their life. By the same usage, the New Testament, because of one point of similarity, will often quote the Old Testament.

iv. Summation – *Sod*

The fourth category is "summation" or "summary." An example of the fourth category is found in Matthew 2:22-23.

> ^{22} *and being warned of God in a dream, he withdrew into the parts of Galilee,* ^{23} *and came and dwelt in a city called Nazareth; that it might be fulfilled which was spoken through the prophets, that he should be called a Nazarene.*

The apparent quotation is *he should be called a Nazarene*, but no such statement is to be found anywhere in the Old Testament. Some have tried to connect this with Isaiah 11:1, but that connection is far-fetched. In verse 23, Matthew uses the plural term *prophets*, so at least two references might be expected, but there is not even one. The fourth category does not directly quote from the Old Testament, as with the first three, but instead *summarizes* what the Old Testament taught. The clue is when the word "prophet" is used in the plural, as it is here. In the first three categories, the word "prophet" is, in most cases, used in the singular. In the fourth category, it is used in the plural, "spoken through the *prophets*." The author is not quoting any specific prophet, but summarizing what the prophets said. In this case, the prophets said that *he should be called a Nazarene*.

What was a Nazarene? In the first century, Nazarenes were a despised people. The term was used to reproach and to shame. This attitude is reflected in John 1:45–46:

> *⁴⁵ Philip finds Nathanael, and says unto him, We have found him, of whom Moses in the law, and the prophets, wrote, Yeshua of Nazareth, the son of Joseph. ⁴⁶ And Nathanael says unto him, Can any good thing come out of Nazareth? Philip says unto him, Come and see.*

Nathanael's question "Can any good thing come out of Nazareth?" is a reflection of the low opinion people had of Nazarenes. Nazarenes were despised and rejected. And what did the Prophets say about the Messiah? They did predict that He would be a despised and rejected individual. The specific term "Nazarene" is a convenient way of summarizing this teaching; not a quotation as such, but a *summary*.

Another example of this category is Luke 18:31–33:

> *³¹ And he took unto him the twelve, and said unto them, Behold, we go up to Jerusalem, and all the things that are written through the prophets shall be accomplished unto the Son of man. ³² For he shall be delivered up unto the Gentiles, and shall be mocked, and shamefully treated, and spit upon: ³³ and they shall scourge and kill him: and the third day he shall rise again.*

Again, note the use of the plural term "prophets." What the Prophets said about the Messiah included nine things: the Messiah will go up to Jerusalem; He will fall into the hands of priests and scribes; the Jewish people will condemn Him to death; they will turn Him over to the Gentiles; the Gentiles will mock Him; they will spit on Him; they will scourge Him; they will kill Him; and He will be resurrected on the third day. No individual prophet said *all* of this. No such quotation exists anywhere in the Prophets. However the Prophets, taken together, did say all of these things, so this is not a direct quotation, but a *summary*.

One more example of this fourth category is Matthew 26:54–56:

> *⁵⁴ How then should the scriptures be fulfilled, that thus it must be? ⁵⁵ In that hour said Yeshua to the multitudes, Are ye come out as against a robber with swords and staves to seize me? I sat daily in the temple teaching, and ye took me not. ⁵⁶ But all this is come to pass, that the scriptures of the prophets might be fulfilled. Then all the disciples left him, and fled.*

Although *Yeshua* taught the people in clear language within the Temple Compound, they rejected Him. This rejection is now obvious in that they are in the garden of Gethsemane, ready to arrest Him. He said that all this has to come to pass *that the scriptures of the prophets might be fulfilled*. No single prophet prophesied what was happening there in the words that *Yeshua* used. But the Prophets together did say that the Messiah would be rejected. He would be arrested and undergo a trial. Just one passage alone, Isaiah 53, is a good example of this. But here, *Yeshua* is not quoting a specific prophecy, but is summarizing what the Prophets did say. In summary, the prophets certainly did teach what *Yeshua* is saying here. Again, this is the fourth category: *summation*.

It is important to understand when studying the Scriptures that every Old Testament quotation in the New Testament will fall into one of these four categories. We simply have to go back to the context of the Old Testament passage, see what it's saying, and then we will know in which category it falls. Therefore, the way the New Testament quotes the Old being used as an objection against plenary verbal inspiration can be refuted by a clear understanding of these four kind of quotations.

e. Conclusion

The conclusion to this study of the relationship of the Bible to the concept of the inspiration of Scripture can be stated in 13 points. First, all Scripture is God-breathed (II Tim. 3:16). Second, it is the Word of God to man (Jn. 10:35). Third, it is infallible (Ps. 19:7). Fourth, it is without error (Prov. 30:5-6). Fifth, it is as it was originally given (II Pet. 1:21). Sixth, it is divinely inspired, and that divine inspiration is plenary (Rom. 15:4). Seventh, it is verbally inspired (Mat. 4:4). Eighth, it is confluent (II Sam. 23:2). Ninth, it is the very words of God, possessing all of His authority (Is. 1:2). Tenth, it is sufficient to save sinners (II Tim. 3:15). Eleventh, it has clarity for understanding (Ps. 119:105). Twelfth, it has the efficacy of convicting sinners (Heb. 4:12). Thirteenth, the central purpose of Scripture is to confess and witness to the Messiah (Lk. 24:44).[28]

In summary, we conclude that the Bible is the Word of God, inspired plenarily, verbally, infallibly, and without error. The Bible is an absolutely reliable source for exactly what God wants man to know, what God wants man to believe, and how God wants the believer to act in his spiritual life.[29]

---

[28] Question 4 on page 67

[29] Suggestion 1 on page 67

C. Questions and Study Suggestions

Question 1: Before going through the theories of inspiration which follow in the next section, how would you explain dual authorship?

Question 2: How does dual authorship answer these false theories?

Question 3: Take a minute to list the *Five Things Plenary Verbal Inspiration Did Not Accomplish* and the *Five Things Plenary Verbal Inspiration Did Accomplish*. Is this description consistent with what is written in II Timothy 3:16-17 and II Peter 1:21?

Question 4: Read each passage in relation to the thirteen points about the inspiration of the Scriptures. Given the understanding of dual authorship and addressing the false theories on the inspiration of the Scriptures, are there points about this study of the relationship of the Bible to the concept of inspiration that you are wrestling with at this point? Are there points of clarity that have come during this study?

Suggestion 1: Take the online test for this section of the study of the Word of God found on http://ariel.org/come-and-see.htm under "The Inspiration of the Scriptures (037)," quiz.

The Word of God

Chapter V

The Covenants of the Bible

Since much of God's relationship to man is based upon covenantal relationships, a study of the eight covenants is a very important aspect of correctly understanding Scripture. The most common way to divide the Bible is by dispensations. The dispensations, however, are based on specific covenants, and knowledge of these covenants will help Bible readers to *rightly divide the word of truth* (II Tim. 2:15). Although the dispensations may come to an end, the covenants themselves often continue.

A. The Types of Covenants

There are two types of covenants in the Bible: conditional and unconditional. It is important to distinguish between these two types of covenants in order to have a clear picture of what the Bible teaches.

A conditional covenant is a bilateral covenant in which a proposal of God to man is characterized by the formula, "If you will, then I will," whereby God promises to grant special blessings to man providing man fulfills certain conditions contained in the covenant. Man's failure to do so often results in punishment. Thus one's response to the covenant agreement brings either blessings or cursings. The blessings are secured by obedience, and man must meet his conditions before God will meet His.

An unconditional covenant is a unilateral covenant and is a sovereign act of God whereby He unconditionally obligates Himself to bring to pass definite blessings and conditions for the covenanted people. This covenant is characterized by the formula, "I will," which declares God's determination to do as He promises. Blessings are secured by the grace of God. There may be conditions in the covenant which God requests the covenanted one to fulfill out of gratitude, but they are not themselves the basis of God's fulfilling His promises.

B. THE COVENANTS WITH ISRAEL

The Bible contains eight covenants. Two of them are conditional: the Edenic and the Mosaic. The other six are unconditional: the Adamic, the Noahic, the Abrahamic, the Land, the Davidic, and the New Covenants.

Five of these eight covenants were made exclusively with Israel while the others were made with mankind in general. Only one of the five covenants made with Israel is conditional: the Mosaic Covenant. The other four covenants with Israel are all unconditional: the Abrahamic Covenant, the Land Covenant, the Davidic Covenant, and the New Covenant.

In light of the above, there are four features of unconditional covenants as they relate to Israel. First, they are literal covenants, with contents which are to be interpreted literally. Second, they are eternal covenants and thus not conditioned by time. Third, they are unconditional covenants. They are not dependent upon Israel's perfect obedience. In fact, these very covenants often make provision for Israel's disobedience. But, since they depend solely upon God for their fulfillment, they can be expected to have total fulfillment. They are unconditional. Fourth, they are made with a covenanted people, *who are Israelites; whose is the adoption, and the glory, and the covenants, and the giving of the law, and the service of God, and the promises* (Romans 9:4).

This passage clearly points out that these covenants were made with the covenanted people and are Israel's possession.

This is brought out again in Ephesians 2:11-12:

[11] Wherefore remember, that once ye, the Gentiles in the flesh, who are called Uncircumcision by that which is called Circumcision, in the flesh, made by hands; [12] that ye were at that time separate from Messiah, alienated from the commonwealth of Israel, and strangers from the covenants of the promise, having no hope and without God in the world.

As mentioned before, five of the eight Bible covenants belong to the people of Israel, and, as this passage notes, Gentiles were considered *strangers from the covenants of the promise*. Four features of these unconditional covenants are: they are literal covenants, they are eternal, they are unconditional, and they are made with a covenanted people.

A covenant can be signed, sealed, and made at a specific point of history, but this does not mean that all the provisions go immediately into effect. In fact, three different things happen once a covenant is sealed: first, some provisions go into effect right away; second, some provisions go into effect in the near future, which may be twenty-five years away or four hundred years away; and third, some provisions go into effect only in the distant prophetic future, not having been fulfilled to this day.[30]

C. The Edenic Covenant

That God had a covenantal relationship with Adam is stated in Hosea 6:7:

But they like Adam have transgressed the covenant: there have they dealt treacherously against me.

The details of the Edenic Covenant are found in Genesis 1:28-30 and 2:15-17.

1. The Participants in the Covenant

The Edenic Covenant was made between God and Adam in that Adam stood as the representative head of the human race. Thus, the actions of Adam are attributed to the whole of humanity.

2. The Provisions of the Covenant

Altogether, there were seven provisions in the Edenic Covenant. The first provision is found in Genesis 1:28a: *And God blessed them: and God said unto them, Be fruitful, and multiply, and replenish the earth.* The earth was created for the purpose of being the habitation of man, and then man was created on the sixth

---

[30] Question 1 and Suggestion 1 on page 116

day. Man was told to populate the earth, so the increase in population is part of his commission. The earth was to be filled with humanity.

The second provision is in verse 28b, where man was told to *subdue* the earth. Previously, authority over the earth had been given to Satan (Ezek. 28:11-19). But when Satan fell, he lost his authority over this earth. That is the reason Genesis 1:2 describes the earth as being covered by water and *darkness was upon the face of the deep*. Hence, God began to form and fashion the earth anew to make it habitable for man, and this time, He would give man the authority over the earth. Man was to use the natural resources and energies of the earth that God had provided for him. However, this did not mean he was allowed to pollute it!

The third provision is given in verse 28c: *and have dominion over the fish of the sea, and over the birds of the heavens, and over every living thing that moves upon the earth.* Man was given *dominion* over all living things. The earlier provision gave man authority over the earth as far as non-living things were concerned. This provision extended man's authority over all living creatures. The entire animal kingdom on the earth, in the air, and in the sea, was put under the authority of man. The first exercise of this authority was man's naming of the animals (Gen. 2:19-20).

The fourth provision, found in Genesis 1:29-30 and 2:16, concerned man's diet:

^{29} And God said, Behold, I have given you every herb yielding seed, which is upon the face of all the earth, and every tree, in which is the fruit of a tree yielding seed; to you it shall be for food: ^{30} and to every beast of the earth, and to every bird of the heavens, and to everything that creeps upon the earth, wherein there is life, I have given every green herb for food: and it was so.

* * *

And Jehovah God commanded the man, saying, Of every tree of the garden you may freely eat: . . .

At this point, man was to be a vegetarian. There is nothing in this covenant that allowed him to eat of the animal kingdom even though he was to exercise authority over it. No blood of any kind was to be shed.

The fifth provision, in Genesis 2:15, concerns man's duties in the garden: *And Jehovah God took the man, and put him into the Garden of Eden to dress it and to keep it.* Man is directed *to dress* and *to keep* the Garden of Eden. Even in his unfallen state, man was not to lead a life of pure leisure; work was part of the human ethic even before the fall. However, labor was easy and the land would produce easily; it was not toilsome.

The sixth provision is found in verse 17a: *but of the tree of the knowledge of good and evil, you shall not eat of it.* Man was forbidden to eat of *the tree of the knowledge of good and evil.* This was the only negative commandment in the entire Edenic Covenant and was the one point that would test man's obedience. He was free to eat of all the other trees of the garden but was to refrain from eating of that one. Man was not to assume that because he was given authority over the earth and the animal kingdom that he himself was independent of God and exempt from God's law. This raises the question, "Will man, like Satan before him, reject God's right to rule and declare himself independent of God?"

The seventh provision contained a penalty for disobedience in verse 17b: *for in the day that you eat thereof you shall surely die.* This cannot refer to physical death because man did not die on the very day that he disobeyed the commandment. So the death spoken of here must be spiritual death. In the day that he eats of *the tree of the knowledge of good and evil,* he will be separated from God and will die spiritually.

3. Basis for a Dispensation and Present Status

The Edenic Covenant became the basis for the first dispensation: the Dispensation of Innocence.

The record of the Edenic Covenant being broken is found in Genesis 3:1-8:

¹ Now the serpent was more subtle than any beast of the field which Jehovah God had made. And he said unto the woman, Yea, has God said, Ye shall not eat of any tree of the garden? ² And the woman said unto the serpent, Of the fruit of the trees of the garden we may eat: ³ but of the fruit of the tree which is in the midst of the garden, God has said, Ye shall not eat of it, neither shall ye touch it, lest ye die. ⁴ And the serpent said unto the woman, Ye shall not surely die: ⁵ for God does know that in the day ye eat thereof, then your eyes shall be opened, and ye shall be as God, knowing good and evil. ⁶ And when the woman saw that the tree was good for food, and that it was a delight to the eyes, and that the tree was to be desired to make one wise, she took of the fruit thereof, and did eat; and she gave also unto her husband with her, and he did eat. ⁷ And the eyes of them both were opened, and they knew that they were naked; and they sewed fig-leaves together, and made themselves aprons. ⁸ And they heard the voice of Jehovah God walking in the garden in the cool of the day: and the man and his wife hid themselves from the presence of Jehovah God amongst the trees of the garden.

Satan appeared in the Garden of Eden as a fallen creature. This shows that man was not created in a perfect universe, for sin was already in existence. Although it was not yet existent in man, it was already present in Satan. The devil did his work of tempting man in the same three areas as set forth in I John 2:16:

I John 2:16	Genesis 3:6
the lust of the flesh	*And when the woman saw that the tree was good for food,*
the lust of the eyes	*and that it was a delight to the eyes,*
and the vainglory [pride] *of life*	*and that the tree was to be desired to make one wise,*

Eve gave in to the temptation and disobeyed the one negative commandment. Adam recognized what had happened, but he still chose to join his wife in disobedience.

According to verse eight, their first reaction was an attempt to hide from the presence of God, which only illustrated the truth of Genesis 2:17. Man at that very moment died spiritually and could no longer share the same communion with God he had experienced before his disobedience. With that act, the Edenic Covenant, being conditional, came to an end.[31]

D. THE ADAMIC COVENANT

The second covenant is the Adamic Covenant, which is found in Genesis 3:14-19.

1. The Participants in the Covenant

As with the first covenant, the second was also made between God and Adam; once again Adam stood as the representative head of the human race. Thus, the judgment on Adam is the judgment on all humanity.

---

[31] Question 2 on page 116

2. The Provisions of the Covenant

God individually addressed the serpent, Satan, Eve, and Adam.

a. The Serpent: Genesis 3:14

> *And Jehovah God said unto the serpent, Because you have done this, cursed are you above all cattle, and above every beast of the field; upon your belly shall you go, and dust shall you eat all the days of your life:*

There are three provisions concerning the serpent. First, he is cursed above all other creatures of the animal kingdom. All creatures now fall under a curse, but there is a special curse upon this one member of the animal kingdom. Normally, an animal is not held morally responsible for its actions. However, if it causes any harm to man, then it is held responsible (Gen. 9:5). Animals were created for the benefit of man, and when this principle is violated, it then incurs God's judgment.

Second, the serpent is to crawl on its belly. This shows that originally the serpent moved in an erect position. This has led to the debate whether or not the serpent originally had legs, but that question is irrelevant to the issue. The only point is that in place of moving erectly, the serpent now crawls on its belly.

Third, *dust* shall be the serpent's food. Bible critics have had a field day with this, pointing it out as an error of the Bible since reptiles do not eat dust. However, this was simply a Hebrew idiom meaning to be especially cursed (Mic. 7:17). The curse will continue to be there even in the Messianic Kingdom (Is. 65:25).[32]

b. Satan: Genesis 3:15

> *I will put enmity between you and the woman, and between your seed and her seed: he shall bruise your head, and you shall bruise his heel.*

Four provisions are given in regard to Satan. First, there would be perpetual hatred between Satan and the woman. Second, this hatred was to culminate between Satan's seed, the Antichrist, and the woman's Seed, the Messiah. Third, the serpent would *bruise* the *heel* of the woman's Seed; this happened at the Crucifixion. Fourth, this first prophecy of the Lord's victory over Satan goes on to say that the woman's Seed will crush Satan's *head*; this occurred initially with the Resurrection

---

[32] Question 3 on page 116

(Heb. 2:14-15). But the final crushing of Satan was still future when Paul wrote Romans 16:20; it will come when Satan is cast into the Lake of Fire (Rev. 20:10).

The main point of this prophecy is that the Messiah would be of the Seed of the woman. This goes against the biblical norm in that genealogy is traced through the male line, not through the female line. The reason for this exception will not be known until centuries later, when Isaiah 7:14 revealed that the Messiah will be conceived through the Holy Spirit and born of a virgin. The prophecy of Genesis 3:15 led to the events of Genesis 6:1-4, when Satan tried to corrupt the Seed of the woman, and will lead to the future supernatural conception of the Antichrist.[33]

c. The Woman: Genesis 3:16

Unto the woman he said, I will greatly multiply your pain and your conception; in pain you shall bring forth children; and your desire shall be to your husband, and he shall rule over you.

Eve and all women were made subject to three provisions. First, there would be multiplication of menstrual *pain* and *conception*. Apparently, the nature of conception before the fall was quite different from what it was after the fall. Since the fall, a woman is generally able to conceive at least once a month. Furthermore, a woman's menstrual periods are accompanied with discomfort and pain.

Second, the woman was to give birth in pain. Eve would have been able to conceive and give birth without pain before the fall, but this was no longer true. However, once birth takes place, there is joy (Jn. 16:21). In this way, the woman is saved (I Tim. 2:15). She is not spiritually saved through childbirth, but she is saved from being in a demeaning position through her ability to produce children, for in this way, she guarantees the continuity of the human race.

Third, the wife was to be in subjection to her husband. This was already true before the fall, but the new element was that she would now have a desire to rebel against that subjection and choose to try to rule him.

d. The Man: Genesis 3:17-19

[17] And unto Adam he said, Because you have hearkened unto the voice of your wife, and have eaten of the tree, of which I commanded you, saying, You shall not eat of it: cursed is the ground for your sake; in toil shall you eat of it all the

---

[33] Question 4 on page 116

days of your life; [18] *thorns also and thistles shall it bring forth to you; and you shall eat the herb of the field;* [19] *in the sweat of your face shall you eat bread, till you return unto the ground; for out of it were you taken: for dust you are, and unto dust shall you return.*

Adam, all men, and the entire human race were subjected to the five provisions in Genesis 3:17-19. First, since Adam stands as the representative head of the human race, the judgment on Adam is the judgment on the whole human race. It is Adam, not Eve, who is held responsible for the human condition.

Second, the earth was cursed. Working was not something new with the Adamic Covenant; it had already been provided for in the previous covenant. The difference was in the earth's response. Under the Edenic Covenant, the earth was to respond readily to man's working and tilling. But now the earth would not respond so easily; there would be *thorns* and *thistles*.

Third, the human diet continued to be vegetarian as it was under the Edenic Covenant; it is not clear if the same was true for the animal kingdom. Animals were used for dairy products, for clothing, and for sacrifices, but not for eating.

Fourth, man's work was to be characterized by hard labor. Working conditions under the Edenic Covenant were easy, simple, and enjoyable. Now, *sweat* was to characterize the work of man and labor was to be hard and toilsome.

Fifth, physical death was introduced. Whereas under the Edenic Covenant man died spiritually, under the Adamic Covenant man would ultimately die physically (Rom. 5:12-21). Thus far, there have only been two exceptions to this rule: Enoch and Elijah. There will be others in the future, at the time of the Rapture.

3. Basis for a Dispensation and Present Status

The Adamic Covenant is the basis for the Dispensation of Conscience. This covenant is unconditional, and so it is still very much in effect.[34]

---

[34] Question 5 on page 116

E. THE NOAHIC COVENANT

The third covenant is called the Noahic Covenant, and it is found in Genesis 9:1-17.

1. The Participants in the Covenant

This covenant was made between God and Noah. Like Adam, Noah stood as the representative for the entire human race. As a result of the Flood, not only is all humanity descended from Adam, but also from Noah.

2. The Provisions of the Covenant

The first provision, found in verses one and seven, is that man was to repopulate the earth:

> *¹ And God blessed Noah and his sons, and said unto them, Be fruitful, and multiply, and replenish the earth.*
>
> * * *
>
> *⁷ And you, be ye fruitful, and multiply; bring forth abundantly in the earth, and multiply therein.*

With the exception of eight people, the Flood destroyed the entire human race. Man had vastly increased in numbers, but *the wickedness of man was great in the earth* (Gen. 6:5). Thus God brought universal judgment upon the earth. After the Flood, the earth was essentially empty again. Only eight people remained to repopulate the entire earth. Just as with the Edenic Covenant, man was again commissioned to repopulate the earth, but the command to subdue the earth is not repeated. With man's fall, he lost his authority, and Satan usurped it. Thus, Satan is *the prince of this world* (Jn. 12:31) and *the god of this world* (II Cor. 4:4). Satan has authority over all the kingdoms of this world and can offer them to whomever he wills (Lk. 4:6). He made that offer to the Seed of the woman, *Yeshua*, who turned it down. He will offer it someday to the seed of Satan, the Antichrist, who will accept it (Rev. 13:1-3).

The second provision is that the fear of man was put into animals and man was to dominate them, as it says in verse 2:

And the fear of you and the dread of you shall be upon every beast of the earth, and upon every bird of the heavens; with all wherewith the ground teems, and all the fishes of the sea, into your hand are they delivered.

While man had lost authority over the earth, he was still to dominate and have authority over the animal kingdom. The fear of man was placed in animals as a means of self-preservation due to the next provision.

The third provision, found in verse 3, is that man's diet was to consist of both moving things and green herbs: *Every moving thing that lives shall be food for you; as the green herb have I given you all.* Previously, his diet had been vegetarian, but now all animals were included. No limitations whatsoever are given in the passage, thus all animals were fit for food.

The fourth provision is that man was forbidden to eat blood, according to verse 4: *But flesh with the life thereof, which is the blood thereof, shall ye not eat.* All creature-life, both man and animal, are blood-sustained. Blood is the symbol of life, and the shedding of blood is the symbol of death. Because blood is the symbol of life, God commanded that it not be eaten or drunk.

The fifth provision is that capital punishment became a part of the human economy for the first time, according to verses 5-6:

⁵ And surely your blood, the blood of your lives, will I require; at the hand of every beast will I require it: and at the hand of man, even at the hand of every man's brother, will I require the life of man. ⁶ Whoso sheds man's blood, by man shall his blood be shed: for in the image of God made he man.

When Cain killed Abel, Cain was not executed because capital punishment had not yet been instituted (Gen. 4:1-15). The provision for capital punishment came with the Noahic Covenant, and all murderers were to be executed.

The sixth provision, the promise that a worldwide flood would never destroy humanity again, is found in verses 8-11:

⁸ And God spoke unto Noah, and to his sons with him, saying, ⁹ And I, behold, I establish my covenant with you, and with your seed after you; ¹⁰ and with every living creature that is with you, the birds, the cattle, and every beast of the earth with you; of all that go out of the ark, even every beast of the earth. ¹¹ And I will establish my covenant with you; neither shall all flesh be cut off any more by the waters of the Flood; neither shall there any more be a flood to destroy the earth.

While there would be local floods that would destroy portions of humanity, never again would there be a worldwide flood. In the future, there will be a passing away and destruction of earth's present system, but it will not be by means of a universal flood. This shows that the Noahic Flood was universal, not local.

The seventh provision, in verses 12-17, is the token of the covenant, the rainbow:

> [12] And God said, This is the token of the covenant which I make between me and you and every living creature that is with you, for perpetual generations: [13] I do set my bow in the cloud, and it shall be for a token of a covenant between me and the earth. [14] And it shall come to pass, when I bring a cloud over the earth, that the bow shall be seen in the cloud, [15] and I will remember my covenant, which is between me and you and every living creature of all flesh; and the waters shall no more become a flood to destroy all flesh. [16] And the bow shall be in the cloud; and I will look upon it, that I may remember the everlasting covenant between God and every living creature of all flesh that is upon the earth. [17] And God said unto Noah, This is the token of the covenant which I have established between me and all flesh that is upon the earth.

Not every covenant came with a sign or token, but this one did. This was the first time in human history that the rainbow ever appeared. Rain did not exist before the worldwide flood, and the earth was watered by a mist that came daily upon the vegetation (Gen. 2:6). Rainbows come in conjunction with rain. So for the first time in human experience a rainbow appeared, and God's promise that humanity will not be destroyed by a flood again should come to remembrance every time a rainbow is seen.

3. Basis for a Dispensation and Present Status:

The Noahic Covenant is the basis for the third dispensation: the Dispensation of Human Government. Now that man is given the authority to shed the blood of a murderer, this requires governmental authority over that individual. God did not sanction anarchy or personal vengeance, but He did sanction capital punishment through a proper carrying out of justice. This requires the concept of human government, and the Noahic Covenant became the basis for it.

We should note at this point that sometimes there can be a dispensation that was based upon a certain covenant, and while the dispensation comes to an end, the covenant itself continues beyond the dispensation. Although the Dispensation of Human Government has been superseded, the unconditional Noahic Covenant is still very much in effect. The judgments of the Tribulation against the Gentiles will come because of violations of the Noahic Covenant. According to Isaiah 24:5-6, the judgment comes because humanity has violated *the everlasting covenant*, a name given to the Noahic Covenant in Genesis 9:16. For that reason, the prophet used the Noahic flood motif, *the windows on high* and *foundations of the earth*, in Isaiah 24:18. The next time God destroys the masses of humanity, it will be by fire.[35]

This was an unconditional covenant and is therefore still very much in effect. The Dispensation of Human Government ended, but this covenant is still valid.

F. THE ABRAHAMIC COVENANT

Genesis 12:1-3 states:

> [1] *Now Jehovah said unto Abram, Get you out of your country, and from your kindred, and from your father's house, unto the land that I will show you:* [2] *and I will make of you a great nation, and I will bless you, and make your name great; and be you a blessing:* [3] *and I will bless them that bless you, and him that curses you will I curse: and in you shall all the families of the earth be blessed.*

Verse 7 says the following:

> *And Jehovah appeared unto Abram, and said, Unto your seed will I give this land: and there built he an altar unto Jehovah, who appeared unto him.*

Genesis 13:14-17 states:

> [14] *And Jehovah said unto Abram, after that Lot was separated from him, Lift up now your eyes, and look from the place where you are, northward and southward and eastward and westward:* [15] *for all the land which you see, to you will I give it, and to your seed forever.* [16] *And I will make your seed as the dust of the earth: so that if a man can number the dust of the earth, then may your seed also be numbered.* [17] *Arise, walk through the land in the length of it and in the breadth of it; for unto you will I give it.*

The fourth and fifth passages dealing with the Abrahamic Covenant are Genesis 15:1-21 and Genesis 17:1-21. While not quoted in this study, these more lengthy segments of Scripture contain many provisions of the Abrahamic Covenant.

---

[35] Question 6 on page 116

The emphasis of Genesis 15 is threefold: first, Abraham would father one nation in particular; second, he would father many nations in general; third, God signs and seals the Abrahamic Covenant and spells out the exact borders described in it as extending from *the river of Egypt* in the south to *the great river* Euphrates in the north. The signing was done in such a way that the covenant was rendered unconditional. The emphasis of Genesis 17 is on the token of the covenant: physical circumcision on the eighth day of a boy's life. Just as the rainbow was the token of the Noahic Covenant, so circumcision is the token of the Abrahamic Covenant.

A sixth passage is Genesis 22:15-18:

> [15] *And the angel of Jehovah called unto Abraham a second time out of heaven,* [16] *and said, By myself have I sworn, says Jehovah, because you have done this thing, and have not withheld your son, your only son,* [17] *that in blessing I will bless you, and in multiplying I will multiply your seed as the stars of the heavens, and as the sand which is upon the sea-shore; and your seed shall possess the gate of his enemies;* [18] *and in your seed shall all the nations of the earth be blessed; because you have obeyed my voice.*

1. The Participants in the Covenant

The persons involved in this covenant were God and Abraham. Abraham stands as the representative head of the entire Jewish nation.

2. The Provisions of the Covenant

A total of fourteen provisions can be deduced from these passages:

1) *A great nation* was to come out of Abraham, namely, the nation of Israel (Gen. 12:2; 13:16; 15:5; 17:1-2, 7; 22:17b).
2) Abraham was promised a land; specifically, *the land of Canaan* (Gen. 12:1, 7; 13:14-15, 17; 15:17-21; 17:8).
3) Abraham himself was to be greatly blessed (Gen. 12:2b).
4) Abraham's name would be great (Gen. 12:2c).
5) Abraham will be a blessing to others (Gen. 12:2d).
6) Those who bless Israel will be blessed (Gen. 12:3a).
7) Those who curse Israel will be cursed (Gen.12:3b).
8) In Abraham all will ultimately be blessed (Gen. 12:3c; 22:18).

9) Abraham would receive a son through his wife Sarah (Gen. 15:1-4; 17:16-21).

10) His descendants would experience the Egyptian bondage (Gen. 15:13-14).

11) Other nations as well as Israel would come forth from Abraham (Gen. 17:3-4, 6); the Arab states are some of these nations.

12) His name was to be changed from Abram, meaning "exalted father," to Abraham, meaning "father of a multitude" (Gen. 17:5).

13) Sarai's name, meaning "my princess," was to be changed to Sarah, meaning "the princess" (Gen. 17:15).

14) Circumcision was to be the token of the covenant (Gen. 17:9-14); thus, according to the Abrahamic Covenant, circumcision was to be a sign of one's Jewishness. The practice of circumcision did not begin with Abraham, since others in the ancient Near East practiced the ritual either at birth or puberty. The uniqueness of Jewish circumcision is not the act, but the timing of the act: on the eighth day. Circumcision would show this to be a blood-covenant and hence emphasized its solemnity. It would also show that this sign of Jewishness is passed on through genealogical history.

These provisions of the Abrahamic Covenant can be categorized in three areas: to Abraham, to the seed (Israel), and to the Gentiles.

a. Abraham

Abraham was to be the father of a great nation, Israel. He was to possess all of the Promised Land. Other nations, including the Arab states, were ultimately to descend from Abraham. Many of his descendants would become kings—both Jewish and non-Jewish kings. Abraham was to receive personal blessings. Abraham was to be a blessing to others. His name was to become great, and so it is among Jews, Muslims, and in all Christendom.

b. Israel

The nation of Israel was to become great. It was ultimately to become innumerable. It was to possess all of the Promised Land. It was to receive victory over its enemies. The fact that these promises were made to both Abraham and his seed shows that these blessings have not yet received complete fulfillment, but await the Messianic Kingdom.

c. Gentiles

The Gentiles would be blessed for blessing Israel and cursed for cursing Israel. Also they were to receive spiritual blessings, but ultimately these were to come through one specific Seed of Abraham, the Messiah. The Abrahamic Covenant contains both physical and spiritual promises. While the physical blessings were limited to the Jews only, the spiritual blessings were to extend to the Gentiles, but only through the Messiah.

3. The Basis for Development of Other Covenants

Reducing the Abrahamic Covenant to its very basics, it can be seen that it contained three main aspects: the land aspect, the seed aspect, and the blessing aspect. The land aspect is developed in the Land Covenant. The seed aspect is covered in the Davidic Covenant. The blessing aspect is presented in the New Covenant.[36]

4. The Confirmation of the Covenant

Abraham had eight sons by three different women, and the question arose, "Through which son would the Abrahamic Covenant be confirmed?" God revealed that it was to be only through Sarah's son, Isaac. God's appearance to Isaac is recorded in Genesis 26:2-5:

> [2] *And Jehovah appeared unto him, and said, Go not down into Egypt; dwell in the land which I shall tell you of:* [3] *sojourn in this land, and I will be with you, and will bless you; for unto you, and unto your seed, I will give all these lands, and I will establish the oath which I swore unto Abraham your father:* [4] *and I will multiply your seed as the stars of heaven, and will give unto your seed all these lands; and in your seed shall all the nations of the earth be blessed;* [5] *because that Abraham obeyed my voice, and kept my charge, my commandments, my statutes, and my laws.*

---

[36] Question 7 on page 116

The covenant was later reconfirmed to Isaac in Genesis 26:24:

And Jehovah appeared unto him the same night, and said, I am the God of Abraham your father: fear not, for I am with you, and will bless you, and multiply your seed for my servant Abraham's sake.

Isaac had two sons, and God chose to confirm the covenant with Jacob, as seen in Genesis 28:13-15:

[13] And, behold, Jehovah stood above it, and said, I am Jehovah, the God of Abraham your father, and the God of Isaac: the land whereon you lie, to you will I give it, and to your seed; [14] and your seed shall be as the dust of the earth, and you shall spread abroad to the west, and to the east, and to the north, and to the south: and in you and in your seed shall all the families of the earth be blessed. [15] And, behold, I am with you, and will keep you whithersoever you go, and will bring you again into this land; for I will not leave you, until I have done that which I have spoken to you of.

The Abrahamic Covenant was lastly confirmed through all twelve sons of Jacob (Gen. 49), who fathered the twelve tribes of Israel.

5. Basis for a Dispensation and Present Status

The Abrahamic Covenant became the basis for the Dispensation of Promise. Because it is unconditional, it is still very much in effect even though it has remained largely unfulfilled. The ultimate fulfillment will come during the Kingdom Age. Some examples include: Exodus 2:23-25; 4:24-26; 6:2-8; 32:11-14; Leviticus 26:46; Deuteronomy 34:4; II Kings 13:22-23; I Chronicles 16:15-19; II Chronicles 20:7-8; Nehemiah 9:7-8; Psalm 105:7-12; Luke 1:54-55, 68-73; Galatians 3:15-18; Hebrews 6:13-20. These passages note that the Abrahamic Covenant was the basis for the Exodus, for giving them the Land, for Jewish survival in spite of disobedience, for the coming of the Messiah, for the resurrection of the dead, and for Israel's final redemption and restoration.

The Abrahamic Covenant is a good example of what was stated earlier: that a covenant could be signed and sealed at a specific point of time, but not every provision went immediately into effect; rather, three different things happen. First, some went into effect right away, such as the change of names and circumcision. Second, some provisions went into effect in the near future, for there was a twenty-five-year wait for the birth of Isaac and over a four-hundred-year wait before the conquest of the land. Third, some provisions will go into effect in the prophetic distant future such as the settlement of all of the Promised Land, which has not been fulfilled to this day.

G. The Mosaic Covenant

The Mosaic Covenant contains very extensive detailed information, and the Scriptural account of the covenant extends from Exodus 20:1 to Deuteronomy 28:68.

1. The Participants in the Covenant

The parties involved in this pact were God and Israel. The covenant was made with Israel and not merely with Moses acting as a representative of Israel. This is clearly brought out in Exodus 19:3-8:

> [3] *And Moses went up unto God, and Jehovah called unto him out of the mountain, saying, Thus shall you say to the house of Jacob, and tell the children of Israel:* [4] *Ye have seen what I did unto the Egyptians, and how I bore you on eagles' wings, and brought you unto myself.* [5] *Now therefore, if ye will obey my voice indeed, and keep my covenant, then ye shall be my own possession from among all peoples: for all the earth is mine:* [6] *and ye shall be unto me a kingdom of priests, and a holy nation. These are the words which you shall speak unto the children of Israel.*
>
> [7] *And Moses came and called for the elders of the people, and set before them all these words which Jehovah commanded him.* [8] *And all the people answered together, and said, All that Jehovah has spoken we will do. And Moses reported the words of the people unto Jehovah.*

The covenant was not made with the Gentiles or the Church, but with Israel only, a point also made in Deuteronomy 4:7-8, Psalm 147:19-20, and Malachi 4:4.

2. The Provisions of the Covenant

The key provision of the Mosaic Covenant was the Law of Moses, which contained a total of 613 commandments. Involved in these provisions of the law were blessings for obedience and curses for disobedience. It was signed and sealed by the *Shechinah* Glory, described in Exodus 24:1-11, but signed in such a way that rendered the covenant conditional. So in essence, there are 613 provisions of the covenant—too many to be listed individually here. Instead, seven observations will be made concerning the provisions.

a. The Totality of the Law

As stated earlier, there were a total of 613 specific commandments, not just ten, a rather common misconception. Of these, 365 were negative commandments, things that were forbidden; 248 were positive commandments, things that should be done.

b. The Blessings and Judgments of the Law

This was a conditional covenant, which meant that there would be blessings for obedience, but judgment for disobedience (Ex. 15:26; 19:3-8).

c. The Blood Sacrifice Added

The key element of the entire Mosaic Law was the blood sacrifice, brought out in Leviticus 17:11:

> *For the life of the flesh is in the blood; and I have given it to you upon the altar to make atonement for your souls: for it is the blood that makes atonement by reason of the life.*

There were five different offerings detailed in Leviticus 1-7. The Hebrew word for *atonement* does not mean "the removal of sin" but merely the "covering of sin." While the blood of animals covered the sins of the Old Testament saints, it never took those sins away; only the blood of the Messiah can remove sin (Heb. 10:1-4). However, the blood sacrifice did provide for the forgiveness of sin and the restoration of fellowship.

d. The Diet Restrictions Imposed

For the Jews, some of the provisions of the Noahic Covenant were restricted. Beasts had to be both cloven-hoofed and those that chewed the cud; fish had to have both fins and scales; concerning fowls, no birds of prey were allowed; and concerning insects, only one type of locust was permitted.

e. The Death Penalty Expanded

For the Jews, the Mosaic Covenant added the death penalty for other sins such as idolatry, adultery, cursing God, cursing parents, breaking the Sabbath, and practicing witchcraft.

f. The Sign of the Covenant

The Mosaic Covenant reaffirmed the practice of circumcision (Lev. 12:3), but not for the same reason. Under the Abrahamic Covenant, circumcision was the sign of the covenant, and it was mandatory for Jews only. Under the Mosaic Covenant, circumcision was the means of submission to the Law of Moses. It was mandatory for all Jews as well as for Gentiles who wished to become part of the commonwealth of Israel. That is why Paul warned the Galatian Gentile believers that if they submitted to circumcision, they would be obliged to keep the *whole law*, not just this one commandment (Gal. 5:3).

g. The Token of the Covenant

The token or sign of the Mosaic Covenant was the Sabbath. Concerning the Sabbath, five specific observations can be made.

First, being the token of the Mosaic Covenant, it was a sign between God and Israel; it was a sign that Israel had been set apart by God (Ex. 31:12-17); it was a sign of the Exodus (Deut. 5:12-15; Ezek. 20:10-12); and it was a sign that Jehovah was Israel's God (Ezek. 20:20). Every reason given for the observance of the Sabbath has relevance only to Israel, not to the Gentiles or to the Church.

Second, the Sabbath was not a creation ordinance; it began only with Moses. Genesis 2:1-3 states only what God did on that day, but there is no command to observe that day. The word *sabbath* is not even used in the Genesis account, and that day of the week is just called the *seventh day*. From Adam to Moses, there is no record of keeping the Sabbath by anyone. While God listed a number of obligations upon humanity in the previous covenants, keeping the Sabbath was not one of them. The Book of Job deals with a pre-Mosaic saint, and it, too, mentions many obligations man had toward God, but keeping the Sabbath was not one of them. According to Exodus 16:23-30, Sabbath observance begins with Moses and was made part of the Law of Moses, as stated in Exodus 20:8-11.

Third, the Sabbath was a day of rest, not a day of corporate worship, which is another common misconception. As the Sabbath commandment was further developed in other parts of the Law of Moses, the meaning of "resting on the Sabbath" was largely a matter of prohibitions: no gathering of manna

(Ex. 16:23-30); no traveling (Ex. 16:29); no kindling of fire (Ex. 35:3); and no gathering of wood (Num. 15:32). Outside the law, other prohibitions for the Sabbath included: no burden-bearing (Jer. 17:21); no trading (Amos 8:5); and no marketing (Neh. 10:31; 13:15, 19). Nothing was said about corporate worship. As found in the New Testament, the Sabbath synagogue services originated with the Babylonian Captivity, not with the Law of Moses. While it was not a day of total inactivity, it was to be a day of rest and refreshment from the regular work of the other six days. While the rest itself may have been an act of worship, corporate worship on the Sabbath was not a factor in the Old Testament.

In connection with the Sabbath, the phrase *a holy convocation* is often found. This phrase is sometimes used as the basis for teaching that the Sabbath was a day of corporate worship for all. However, it is used only in conjunction with the priesthood and sacrifices. The corporate connotation is for the priests only, and the place of this corporate worship is in the Tabernacle or Temple for the purpose of sacrifices. Since only the priesthood could do the work of sacrificing, the *holy convocation* applied only to them. This phrase is found a total of 19 times, all in three of the books of Moses: Exodus, Leviticus, and Numbers. Eleven of the 19 times are found in one chapter: Leviticus 23. The phrase is found another six times in the two chapters of Numbers 28-29. In all cases, the phrase *holy convocation* refers to a convocation of priests for the purpose of performing special sacrifices, and the Sabbath was one of those occasions. It was not a time of corporate worship for all Israel. So the one passage that is used to try to substantiate corporate worship on the Sabbath, Leviticus 23:3, refers to the Sabbath as a *holy convocation* and has to do with priestly corporate sacrifices. While it has relevance to family gatherings, these were not acts of corporate worship. Dr. Louis Goldberg of Moody Bible Institute states: "On the Sabbath there was to be complete rest (physical) and holy convocation (spiritual refreshing) before the Lord."[37]

Concerning the Sabbath, even Leviticus 23:3 states: *it is a sabbath unto Jehovah in all your dwellings*. Again, the emphasis has to do with staying at home (Ex. 16:29) and resting as a family, rather than getting together in corporate worship. As Dr. Goldberg also points out, the rest "was also to include spiritual renewal."[38] The expression *holy convocation* emphasized that on such occasions the priests were to offer special sacrifices. In reality, the Mosaic Law mandated corporate worship on

---

[37] Louis A. Goldberg, *Leviticus: A Study Guide Commentary* (Grand Rapids: Zondervan Publishing House, 1980), p. 116.

[38] Ibid., p. 117.

only three occasions: the Feast of Passover, the Feast of Weeks, and the Feast of Tabernacles. On these occasions, they were to migrate to wherever the Tabernacle, or later the Temple, stood, either at Shiloh or Jerusalem. Corporate worship by non-Levites was mandated only three times a year, but not on a weekly Sabbath. This would have been physically impossible in light of the time it took to travel during biblical times. The penalty for profaning the Sabbath was death; to profane the Sabbath was to consider it like any other day. Therefore, on the Sabbath, they were to do no labor, and they were to stay home and rest.

Fourth, the Sabbath as the token or sign of the Mosaic Covenant was intended only for Israel, not the Church.

Fifth, as the sign of the Mosaic Covenant, it is in force as long as the covenant is in force. If the Mosaic Covenant comes to an end, so would mandatory Sabbath-keeping.

3. Relationship to Previous Covenants

The fourth consideration is the relationship of the Mosaic Covenant to the other covenants. We can mention two points.

The Mosaic Covenant limited the dietary law of the Noahic Covenant. Under the Noahic Covenant, a person could eat anything they wanted, without exception. But the Mosaic Covenant limited what may be eaten and what may not be eaten. It introduced limitations in the area of meat, fowl, and fish. But while it limited the diet of the Noahic Covenant for Jews, the Gentiles remained under the Noahic Covenant. They were never placed under the Mosaic Covenant and so could still eat anything they wanted, while Jews now had dietary restrictions.

A second concern is its relationship to the Abrahamic Covenant. The token of the Abrahamic Covenant was circumcision. Under that covenant, circumcision was a sign of Jewishness. But under the Mosaic Covenant, circumcision became the means of submission to the Law of Moses.

4. The Purposes of the Law

It should be stated categorically that the Law of Moses was not a means of salvation. This concept is rejected because that would make salvation by means of works. Salvation was and always is by grace through faith. While the content of faith has changed from age to age depending on progressive revelation, the means of salvation never changes. The law was not given to serve as a means of salvation

(Rom. 3:20, 28; Gal. 2:16; 3:11, 21). It was given to a people already redeemed from Egypt, not in order to redeem them. However, there were at least nine purposes for the Law of Moses, found in both testaments.

a. To Reveal the Holiness of God

The law was to reveal the holiness of God and to reveal the standard of righteousness that God demanded for a proper relationship with Him (Lev. 11:44; 19:1-2, 37; I Pet. 1:15-16). The law itself was *holy, and righteous, and good* (Rom. 7:12).

b. To Provide a Rule of Conduct

The law was to provide the rule of conduct for the Old Testament saints. For example, Romans 3:28 makes it clear that no man was justified by the works of the law. The law always had purposes other than being a means of salvation. In this case, it provided the rule of life for the Old Testament believer (Lev. 11:44-45; 19:2; 20:7-8, 26), more specifically, the Jewish saint since the rule of life for Gentile saints were the Adamic and the Noahic Covenants. The law was the center of his spiritual life and his delight, as stated in Psalm 119, verses 77, 97, 103-104, and 159.

c. To Provide for Corporate Worship

The law was to provide occasions for individual and corporate worship for Israel. The seven holy seasons of Israel (Lev. 23) is one example of this.

d. To Keep Jews a Distinct People

The law was to keep the Jews a distinct people (Lev. 11:44-45; Deut. 7:6; 14:1-2). This was the specific reason for many of the laws, such as the dietary laws and the clothing laws. The Jews were to be distinct from all other people in a variety of ways, such as their worship habits (Lev. 1-7, 16, 23), their eating habits (Lev. 11:1-47), their sexual habits (Lev. 12), their clothing habits (Lev. 19:19), and even the way they cut their beards (Lev. 19:27). Other passages for this point include Exodus 19:5-8 and 31:13.

e. To Serve as a Middle Wall of Partition

The law was to serve as *the middle wall of partition*, as stated in Ephesians 2:11-16. The four unconditional covenants are Jewish covenants and God's blessings, both physical and spiritual, are mediated through the four covenants, the *covenants of the promise* mentioned in verse 12. Because of the Jewish nature of these unconditional covenants, a conditional covenant was also added, the Mosaic Covenant, containing the Law of Moses, the *law of commandments contained in ordinances* of verse 15. The purpose of the law, then, was to become *the middle wall of partition* to keep Gentiles-as-Gentiles from enjoying the Jewish spiritual blessings of the unconditional covenants. Because of this purpose, Gentiles were both *alienated from the commonwealth of Israel, and strangers from the covenants of the promise*. The only way Gentiles could enjoy the spiritual blessings of the Jewish covenants during the period of the law was to take upon themselves the obligation of the law, undergo the rite of circumcision, and then live like every Jew had to live. Gentiles-as-Gentiles could not enjoy the Jewish spiritual blessings, only Gentiles-as-proselytes to Mosaic Judaism.

f. To Reveal Sin

The law was to reveal what sin is. Three passages in the Book of Romans make this point. The first passage is Romans 3:19-20, where Paul emphasized that there is no justification through the law; by means of the law, no Jewish person will be justified. What is the law, then, if not a way of justification, a way of salvation? The law was given to provide the knowledge of sin, to reveal exactly what sin is. The second passage is Romans 5:20, where the law was given so that trespasses might be made very clear. How does one know he has sinned? He knows because the law spelled out in detail what was permitted and what was not permitted. The law with its 613 commandments revealed sin. The third passage is Romans 7:7. Paul again emphasized the fact that the law was given so that sin might be made known. Paul became aware of his sinful state by looking into the law and knowing that on the basis of the law he fell short.

g. To Make One Sin More

The picture Paul gives is that the law came in to actually make one sin more. Romans 4:15 states: *for the law works wrath; but where there is no law, neither is there transgression.*

Paul adds in Romans 5:20: *And the law came in besides, that the trespass might abound; but where sin abounded, grace did abound more exceedingly.*

How this works is explained by Paul in Romans 7:7-13. It is also explained in I Corinthians 15:56, which reads: *The sting of death is sin; and the power of sin is the law.*

Basically, what Paul taught is that the sin-nature needs a base of operation, and that base of operation is the law. When Paul said: *where there is no law, neither is there transgression,* he did not mean, of course, that there was no sin before the law was given. The term *transgression* is a specific type of sin; it is the violation of a specific commandment. Men were sinners before the law was given, but they were not transgressors of the law until the law was given. Once the law was given, the sin-nature had a base of operation, causing the individual to violate these commandments and sin all the more.

h. To Show Man's Inability to Please God

The law was to show the sinner that there was nothing he could do on his own to please God; he had no ability to keep the law perfectly or to attain the righteousness of the law (Rom. 7:14-25).

i. To Drive One to Faith

The law was to bring one to saving faith in the Messiah, according to Romans 8:1-4 and Galatians 3:24-25.

j. Summary

The purposes of the Law of Moses can be categorized in four aspects. First, in relation to God, it was to reveal His holiness and to reveal His righteous standards. Second, in relation to Israel, it was to keep Israel a distinct people, to provide a rule of life for the Old Testament saint and to provide for individual and corporate worship. Third, in relation to Gentiles, it was to serve as a middle wall of partition and thus keep them strangers to the unconditional Jewish covenants so as not to partake of Jewish spiritual blessings as Gentiles, but only as proselytes to Mosaic Judaism. Fourth, in relation to sin, it was to reveal what sin is, to make one sin more, to show that a man cannot attain the righteousness of the law on his own, and to drive one to faith.

5. The Present Status

The Mosaic Covenant was the basis for the Dispensation of Law. It was the one Jewish covenant that was conditional and ultimately came to an end with the death of the Messiah (Rom. 10:4; II Cor. 3:3-11; Gal. 3:19-29; Eph. 2:11-18; Heb. 7:11-12, 18). Hence, the Mosaic Law is no longer in effect. Prophetically, it was already considered broken even before the Messiah died to free the Jew from the penalty of the law (Jer. 31:32). The status of the Mosaic Covenant will be discussed in seven points.

a. The Unity of the Law of Moses

Two factors have developed in the minds and teachings of many believers that have contributed to the confusion over the Law of Moses. One is the practice of dividing the law into "ceremonial," "legal," and "moral" commandments. On the basis of this division, many have come to think that the believer is free from the ceremonial and legal commandments, but is still under the moral commandments. The second factor is the belief that the Ten Commandments are still valid today while the other 603 commandments are not. When confronted by a Seventh-Day Adventist, the individual taking this approach runs into problems concerning the fourth commandment on keeping the Sabbath. At that point, fudging begins to result in inconsistency. It must be understood that the Scriptures view the Mosaic Law as a unit. The word *Torah*, meaning "law," is always singular when applied to the Law of Moses, even though it contains 613 commandments. The same is true of the Greek word *nomos* in the New Testament. The division of the Law of Moses into ceremonial, legal, and moral parts is convenient for the study of the different types of commandments contained within it, but the Scriptures themselves never divide it in this way. Neither is there any scriptural basis for separating the Ten Commandments from the whole 613 and making them perpetual. All 613 commandments are a single unit comprising the Law of Moses.

It is the principle of the unity of the Law of Moses that lies behind the statement found in James 2:10: *For whosoever shall keep the whole law, and yet stumble in one point, he is become guilty of all.* The point is clear. A person needs only to break one of the 613 commandments to be guilty of breaking all of the Law of Moses. This can be true only if the Mosaic Law is a unit. If it is not, the guilt lies only in the particular commandment violated, not in the whole law. In other words, if one breaks a legal commandment, he is guilty of breaking the ceremonial and moral laws as well. The same is true of breaking a moral or ceremonial commandment. To bring the point closer to home, if a person eats ham, according to the Law of Moses, he is guilty of breaking the Ten Commandments, although none of them says anything about eating ham. The law is a unit, and to break one of the 613 commandments is to break them all.

In order to have a clear understanding of the Law of Moses and its relationship to the believer, Jewish or Gentile, it is necessary to view it as the Scriptures view it: a unit that cannot be divided into parts that have been done away with and parts that have not. Nor can certain commandments be separated in such a way as to give them a different status from other commandments.

b. The Law of Moses Has Been Rendered Inoperative

The clear-cut teaching of the New Testament is that the Law of Moses has been rendered inoperative with the death of the Messiah; in other words, the law in its totality no longer has authority over any individual. This is evident from a number of passages.

The first passage is Romans 7:5-6:

> ⁵ *For when we were in the flesh, the sinful passions, which were through the law, wrought in our members to bring forth fruit unto death.* ⁶ *But now we have been discharged from the law, having died to that wherein we were held; so that we serve in newness of the spirit, and not in oldness of the letter.*

Paul declares that the believer has been *discharged from the law*. The Greek word used is *katargeo*, which means, "to render inoperative." The law has been rendered inoperative insofar as being the rule of life for the believer.

The second passage is Romans 10:4: *For Messiah is the end of the law unto righteousness to every one that believes.* The Greek word for *end* is *telos* and can mean either "termination" or "goal." However, the evidence clearly favors the meaning of *end* as "termination." The Messiah is the goal of the law, but He is also the termination of the law. Since the Messiah is the *end of the law*, this means that there is no justification through it (Gal. 2:16). This, of course, was always true but, furthermore, there is no sanctification or perfection through the law (Heb. 7:19). Thus it should be very evident that the law has come to an end in the Messiah and cannot function in justification or sanctification. It has been rendered inoperative, especially for the believer.

The third passage is Galatians 3:19: *What then is the law? It was added because of transgressions, till the seed should come to whom the promise has been made.* The law was never meant to be a permanent administration, only a temporary one. In this context, Paul stated that the Law of Moses was an addition to the Abrahamic Covenant (vv. 15-18). It was added for the purpose of making sin very clear so that all will know that they have fallen short of God's standard of righteousness. It was a temporary addition until the *seed*, the Messiah, would come. Now that He has come, the law is finished; the addition has ceased to function with the cross.

The fourth passage is Hebrews 7:11-18:

> ¹¹ *Now if there was perfection through the Levitical priesthood (for under it have the people received the law), what further need was there that another priest should arise after the order of Melchizedek, and not be reckoned after*

> the order of Aaron? ¹² *For the priesthood being changed, there is made of necessity a change also of law.* ¹³ *For he of whom these things are said belongs to another tribe, from which no man has given attendance at the altar.* ¹⁴ *For it is evident that our Lord has sprung out of Judah; as to which tribe Moses spoke nothing concerning priests.* ¹⁵ *And what we say is yet more abundantly evident, if after the likeness of Melchizedek there arises another priest,* ¹⁶ *who has been made, not after the law of a carnal commandment, but after the power of an endless life:* ¹⁷ *for it is witnessed of him, "You are a priest forever after the order of Melchizedek."*

With the Messiah, there is a new priesthood according to the order of Melchizedek, not according to the order of Aaron. The Law of Moses provided the basis for the Levitical priesthood and there was an inseparable connection between the Law of Moses and the Levitical priesthood. Thus, a new priesthood required a new law under which it could operate. The point made in verses 11-12 is that, under the law, only one type of priesthood was permitted, the Levitical priesthood. The Levitical priesthood could not bring perfection. This is explained in Hebrews 9:11-10:18, which states rather clearly that animal blood could not bring perfection; only the Messiah's blood could do that. For the Levitical priesthood to be done away with and to be replaced by a new priesthood, the Priesthood of Melchizedek, required a change of the law. In verses 13-17 it says that, as long as the Law of Moses was in effect, no other priesthood was valid. Was there a change of the law?

The Mosaic Law was "disannulled" according to verse 18: *For there is a disannulling of a foregoing commandment because of its weakness and unprofitableness.* Because it is no longer in effect, there is now a new priesthood after the order of Melchizedek. If the Mosaic Law were still in effect, *Yeshua* could not function as a priest. Because the Mosaic Law is no longer in effect, *Yeshua* can be a priest after the order of Melchizedek. Consequently, the Law of Moses has been "disannulled" in favor of a new law, which is the basis for the priesthood according to the order of Melchizedek.

The fifth passage is Hebrews 8:8-13. The writer of Hebrews goes on to say that the prophets already anticipated the above truth. In verses 8-12, he quotes the New Covenant of Jeremiah 31:31-34 and then concludes in verse 13: *In that he says, A new covenant, he has made the first old. But that which is becoming old and waxed aged is nigh unto vanishing away.* Thus the Law of Moses became *old* with Jeremiah and vanished away with the Messiah's death.

The sixth passage is Ephesians 2:14-15:

14 For he is our peace, who made both one, and broke down the middle wall of partition, 15 having abolished in his flesh the enmity, even the law of commandments contained in ordinances; that he might create in himself of the two one new man, so making peace; . . .

The law was *the middle wall of partition* that was now broken down. As noted earlier, God made four unconditional eternal covenants with Israel. All of God's blessings, both material and spiritual, are mediated by means of these four Jewish covenants. God also made a fifth covenant, which was temporary and conditional, the Mosaic Covenant that contained the Mosaic Law. The Mosaic Law served as *the middle wall of partition* to keep Gentiles-as-Gentiles from enjoying Jewish spiritual blessings. If the Mosaic Law were still in effect, it would still be a wall of partition to keep the Gentiles away; but this wall of partition was broken down with the death of the Messiah. Since the wall of partition was the Mosaic Law, this meant the Law of Moses was done away with. Gentiles-as-Gentiles on the basis of faith can and do enjoy Jewish spiritual blessings by becoming fellow-partakers of the promise in the Messiah.

The seventh passage for the annulment of the Mosaic Law is based on Galatians 3:23-4:7. In verse 24, the law is looked upon as a pedagogue or a tutor over a minor to bring him to mature faith in the Messiah. Having become a believer, according to verse 25, he is no longer under this tutor, which is the Law of Moses. As clearly as it could be stated, this passage teaches that with the Messiah's coming, the law is no longer in effect.

The eighth passage for the annulment of the Mosaic Law is II Corinthians 3:2-11 that zeros right in on the Ten Commandments, the part of the law that most people want to retain. One first needs to see what Paul is saying concerning the Law of Moses. In verses three and seven, the spotlight is on the Ten Commandments, since it is these that were *engraven on stones*. In verse seven, it is called the *ministration of death*. In verse nine, it is called the *ministration of condemnation*. These are negative, but valid, descriptions. The main point, then, is that the Law of Moses, especially represented by the Ten Commandments, is a *ministration of death* and a *ministration of condemnation*. If the Ten Commandments were still in force today, this would still be true. However, they are no longer in force, for it states in verses seven and 11 that the law has "passed away." The Greek word used is *katargeo*, which means, "to render inoperative." Since the emphasis in this passage is on the Ten Commandments, this means that the Ten Commandments have passed away. The thrust is very clear. The Law of

Moses, and especially the Ten Commandments, is no longer in effect. In fact, the superiority of the Law of the Messiah is seen by the fact that it will never be rendered inoperative. Unlike covenant theology, dispensationalism does not insist that the Ten Commandments are still in force and have to do exegetical gymnastics to avoid observing the Sabbath the very way the Ten Commandments actually require.

To summarize this section, the law is a unit comprised of 613 commandments, all of which have been rendered inoperative. There is no commandment that has continued beyond the cross of the Messiah. The law can be used as a teaching tool to show God's standard of righteousness, as well as man's sinfulness and need of a substitutionary atonement. It can be used to teach many spiritual truths about God. It can be used to point one to the Messiah (Gal. 3:23-25). However, it has completely ceased to function as an authority over the individual. It is no longer the rule of life for believers.

c. The Moral Law

It is this part of the Law of Moses that many generally try to retain and conclude therefore that the Law of Moses is still in effect. However, the moral law preceded the Law of Moses. The moral law is not identical to the Law of Moses. Adam and Eve broke the moral law long before Moses. Satan broke the moral law even before Adam. The Law of Moses embodied the moral law, but did not originate it. Now the moral law is embodied in the Law of the Messiah.

d. Matthew 5:17-18

A favorite objection to the teaching of the termination of the Law of Moses is the Messiah's statement in Matthew 5:17-18:

> [17] *Think not that I came to destroy the law or the prophets: I came not to destroy, but to fulfil.* [18] *For verily I say unto you, Till heaven and earth pass away, one jot or one tittle shall in no wise pass away from the law, till all things be accomplished.*

Those who cite this passage are seldom consistent with it. It is obvious that *Yeshua* was speaking of the Law of Moses. Yet those who use this passage never accept their own thesis since they must believe in the doing away in some form of many, if not most, of the commandments of the Law of Moses. The commandments concerning priesthood and sacrifice are only one example; other examples, including the food laws and clothing laws, can be cited. Regardless of what semantics, such as "supersede," "brought to greater fulfillment," "bringing out its true meaning," among others, may be used to describe this change, it is clear that a great many of the 613 commandments no longer apply as they were written. If, by the Law of Moses, they mean only the moral commandments, then their citation of Matthew 5:17-18 does not prove their point. Verse 19 must not be ignored:

> *Whosoever therefore shall break one of these least commandments, and shall teach men So shall be called least in the kingdom of heaven; but whosoever shall do and teach them, he shall be called great in the kingdom of heaven.*

The phrase *these least commandments* include more than merely the moral commandments, the emphasis is on the entire law, all 613 commandments. It is true that *Yeshua* came to fulfill the law. However, the Law of Moses did not end with the coming of the Messiah or by His life; it ended with His death. As long as He was alive, He was under the Mosaic Law and had to fulfill and obey every commandment applicable to Him, not in the way that the rabbis had reinterpreted it. The statement of Matthew 5:17-19 was made while He was living. Even while He was living, He had already implied the doing away with the law. One example is Mark 7:19: *This he said, making all meats clean*. Can it be any clearer than this that at least the dietary commandments have been done away with? Again, all must admit that great parts of the law no longer apply in the manner prescribed by Moses. Have they been done away with or not? To constantly claim that the Law of Moses is still in effect or that it is the same as the Law of the Messiah, while ignoring the details of that same law, is inconsistent and a theological fallacy.

As for the meaning of the word *fulfil*, Matthew consistently uses the Greek term in reference to fulfilling prophecy and so bringing it to an end. Matthew 1:22-23 states that the prophecy of Isaiah 7:14 was fulfilled, that this brought the prophecy to an end and so nothing in the future will fulfill it. To "fulfill" meant to accomplish what prophecy demanded, while to "abolish" meant to fail to accomplish it.

e. The Law of Messiah

The Law of Moses has been disannulled, and believers are now under a new law. This new law is called the *law of Messiah* in Galatians 6:2 and the *law of the Spirit of life* in Romans 8:2. This is a brand-new law, totally separate from the Law of Moses. The Law of the Messiah contains all the individual commandments from the Messiah and the apostles that are applicable to a New Testament believer. The details on this period will be discussed under the New Covenant.

f. The Principle of Freedom

The principle of freedom declares that the believer in the Messiah is free from the Law of Moses. This means that he is free from the necessity of keeping any commandment of that system. On the other hand, he is also free to keep parts of the Law of Moses, if he so desires. The biblical basis for this freedom to keep the law can be seen in the actions of Paul, who was the greatest exponent of freedom from the law. His vow in Acts 18:18 is based on Numbers 6:2, 5, 9, and 18. His desire to be in Jerusalem for Pentecost in Acts 20:16 is based on Deuteronomy 16:16. The strongest passage is Acts 21:17-26, where Paul himself, the apostle of freedom from the law, is seen keeping the law. The believer is free from the law, but he is also free to keep parts of it, those parts that do not violate the principles or commandments of the loving Messiah. Thus, if a Jewish believer feels the need to refrain from eating pork, he is free to do so. The same is true for all the other commandments.

However, there are two dangers that must be avoided by any believer who voluntarily keeps the commandments of the Law of Moses. One danger is the idea that by doing so he is contributing to his own justification and sanctification. This is false. The second danger is in expecting others to keep the same commandments he has decided to keep. This is equally wrong and borders on legalism. The one who exercises his freedom to keep the law must recognize and respect another's freedom not to keep it.

g. The Sabbath

The Sabbath was the sign, seal, and token of the Mosaic Covenant. As long as that covenant was in effect, the Sabbath law was mandatory. Since the Law of Moses has been rendered inoperative, the Sabbath command no longer applies. Those with their inconsistent insistence that the Ten Commandments are still in effect also insist that the Sabbath law applies. However, they totally ignore what Moses wrote about how to keep the Sabbath and they even change the day of the week, something that the Law of Moses does not allow. Many Jewish believers also insist on mandatory Sabbath-keeping. Although they inconsistently base it on the Law of Moses, at least they retain it with the seventh day of the week. The apologetics used for mandatory Sabbath-keeping are almost exclusively based on the Old Testament for obvious reasons: there is no New Testament commandment for believers in general or Jewish believers in particular to keep the Sabbath. The claim that Sabbath observance is part of the New Covenant is nowhere supported by the New Covenant Scriptures themselves. In fact, if anything, they would teach the opposite.

The covenant was not made with the Gentiles or the Church, but with Israel only, a point also made in Deuteronomy 4:7-8; Psalm 147:19-20; and Malachi 4:4.

H. The Land Covenant

For the lack of a better name, this covenant is commonly known as the Palestinian Covenant, for it largely concerns the land known for centuries as Palestine. This is an unfortunate term now for two reasons. First, it was a name given to the land by the Roman Emperor Hadrian after the Second Jewish Revolt under Bar Cochba (A.D. 132-135). His purpose was to erase any Jewish remembrance of the land as part of his policy to "de-Judaize" the land. Second, due to the historical events in the Middle East in the history of modern Israel, the name is associated more with Arabs than with Jews. Perhaps a better title for this covenant would have been the "Land Covenant" since "Palestine" is not a biblical designation anyway. Thus, this study will refer to it as the Land Covenant, but it should be noted that this is the same as that which is called the "Palestinian Covenant" in many books.

Although this covenant is within the fifth book of Moses, Deuteronomy 29:1 clearly shows that the Land Covenant is distinct from the Mosaic Covenant:

These are the words of the covenant which Jehovah commanded Moses to make with the children of Israel in the land of Moab, besides the covenant which he made with them in Horeb.

1. The Participants in the Covenant

This covenant was made between God and Israel, the same two parties as the Mosaic Covenant.

2. The Provisions of the Covenant

Eight provisions can be gleaned from this passage. First, Moses spoke prophetically of Israel's coming disobedience to the Mosaic Law and her subsequent scattering over the entire world (Deut. 29:2-30:1). All remaining provisions speak of various facets of Israel's final restoration.

Second, Israel will repent, as it says in Deuteronomy 30:2: *And shall return unto Jehovah your God, to all that I command you this day, you and your children, with all your heart, and with all your soul.*

Third, the Messiah will return, according to verse 3a: *that then Jehovah your God will turn your captivity.*

Fourth, Israel will be regathered, as it states in verses 3b-4:

³ᵇ and have compassion upon you, and will return and gather you from all the peoples, whither Jehovah your God has scattered you. ⁴ If any of your outcasts be in the uttermost parts of heaven, from thence will Jehovah your God gather you: . . .

Fifth, verse five says Israel will possess the Promised Land: *Jehovah your God will bring you into the land which your fathers possessed, and you shall possess it; and he will do you good, and multiply you above your fathers.*

Sixth, a description of how Israel will be regenerated is in verse six: *And Jehovah your God will circumcise your heart, and the heart of your seed, to love Jehovah your God with all your heart, and with all your soul, that you may live.*

Seventh, the enemies of Israel will be judged in verse seven: *And Jehovah your God will put all these curses upon your enemies, and on them that hate you, that persecuted you.*

Eighth, Israel will receive full blessing; specifically, the blessings of the Messianic Age, enumerated in verses 8-20:

⁸ And you shall return and obey the voice of Jehovah, and do all his commandments which I command you this day. ⁹ And Jehovah your God will make you plenteous in all the work of your hand, in the fruit of your body, and in the fruit of your cattle, and in the fruit of your ground, for good: for Jehovah will again rejoice over you for good, as he rejoiced over your fathers; ¹⁰ if you shall obey the voice of Jehovah your God, to keep his commandments and his statutes which are written in this book of the law; if you turn unto Jehovah your God with all your heart, and with all your soul.

¹¹ For this commandment which I command you this day, it is not too hard for you, neither is it far off. ¹² It is not in heaven, that you should say, Who shall go up for us to heaven, and bring it unto us, and make us to hear it, that we may do it? ¹³ Neither is it beyond the sea, that you should say, Who shall go over the sea for us, and bring it unto us, and make us to hear it, that we may do it? ¹⁴ But the word is very nigh unto you, in your mouth, and in your heart, that you may do it.

[15] *See, I have set before you this day life and good, and death and evil;* [16] *in that I command you this day to love Jehovah your God, to walk in his ways, and to keep his commandments and his statutes and his ordinances, that you may live and multiply, and that Jehovah your God may bless you in the land whither you go in to possess it.* [17] *But if your heart turn away, and you will not hear, but shall be drawn away, and worship other gods, and serve them;* [18] *I denounce unto you this day, that ye shall surely perish; ye shall not prolong your days in the land, whither you pass over the Jordan to go in to possess it.* [19] *I call heaven and earth to witness against you this day, that I have set before you life and death, the blessing and the curse: therefore choose life, that you may live, you and your seed;* [20] *to love Jehovah your God, to obey his voice, and to cleave unto him; for he is your life, and the length of your days; that you may dwell in the land which Jehovah swore unto your fathers, to Abraham, to Isaac, and to Jacob, to give to them.*

3. The Importance of the Covenant

The special importance of the Land Covenant is that it reaffirms the title deed to the land as belonging to Israel. Although she would prove unfaithful and disobedient, the right to the land would never be taken from her. Furthermore, it shows that the conditional Mosaic Covenant did not lay aside the unconditional Abrahamic Covenant. It might be taken by some that the Mosaic Covenant displaced the Abrahamic Covenant, but the Land Covenant shows that this is not true. The Land Covenant is an enlargement of the original Abrahamic Covenant. It amplifies the land aspect and emphasizes the promise of the land to God's earthly Jewish people in spite of their unbelief. The Abrahamic Covenant teaches that ownership of the land is unconditional while the Land Covenant teaches that the enjoyment of the land is conditioned on obedience.

4. The Confirmation of the Covenant: Ezekiel 16:1-63

The Land Covenant received its confirmation centuries later, reflected in Ezekiel 16:1-63. In this very important passage concerning God's relationship to Israel, God recounts His love of Israel in her infancy (vv. 1-7). Later (vv. 8-14) Israel was chosen by God and became related to Jehovah by marriage and hence became the Wife of Jehovah. However, Israel played the harlot and was guilty of spiritual adultery by means of idolatry (vv. 15-34); therefore, it was necessary to punish her by means of dispersion (vv. 35-52). This dispersion is not final, for there would be a future restoration on the basis of the Land Covenant (vv. 53-63). They were guilty of violating the Mosaic Covenant (vv. 53-59), but God will remember the covenant made with Israel in her youth (v. 60a) and will establish an everlasting covenant, the New Covenant (v. 60b), and this will result in Israel's national salvation (vv. 61-63).

5. The Present Status

The Land Covenant, being an unconditional covenant, is still very much in effect.[39]

I. THE DAVIDIC COVENANT

The seventh covenant is called the Davidic Covenant. There are two main Scriptures concerning this covenant. The first passage is in II Samuel 7:11b-17, where the emphasis is on Solomon. The second passage is I Chronicles 17:10-15, where the emphasis is on the Messiah.

1. The Participants in the Covenant

This covenant was made between God and David, who stands as the head of the Davidic house and dynasty, the only rightful claimant to the Davidic throne in Jerusalem.

2. The Provisions of the Covenant

Careful study of both biblical accounts brings out the seven provisions of the Davidic Covenant. First, David is promised an eternal dynasty in II Samuel 7:11b and 16 and I Chronicles 17:10b:

> [11b] *Moreover Jehovah tells you that Jehovah will make you a house.*

* * *

---

[39] Suggestion 2 on page 116

> ¹⁶ *And your house and your kingdom shall be made sure forever before you: your throne shall be established forever.*

* * *

> ¹⁰ᵇ *Moreover I tell you that Jehovah will build you a house.*

Nothing could ever destroy the house of David—it will always be in existence. Although it is unknown who they are, somewhere in the Jewish world, members of the house of David still exist to this day.

Second, one of David's own sons, specifically Solomon, was to be established on the throne after David, according to II Samuel 7:12: *When your days are fulfilled, and you shall sleep with your fathers, I will set up your seed after you, that shall proceed out of your bowels, and I will establish his kingdom.*

Absalom and Adonijah, two of David's other sons, tried to usurp the throne; but Solomon, and Solomon alone, was to be established on David's throne.

Third, verse 13a says that Solomon would build the Temple: *He shall build a house for my name.* Although David had greatly desired to build God's Temple, his hands had shed much blood and he was guilty of murder at one point. Thus, he was forbidden to build the Temple, and the job would rest with his son, Solomon.

Fourth, the throne of David's kingdom was to be established *forever*, according to verses 13b and 16:

> ¹³ᵇ *I will establish the throne of his kingdom forever.*

* * *

> ¹⁶ *And your house and your kingdom shall be made sure forever before you: your throne shall be established forever*

It was not Solomon himself who was promised to be established *forever*; rather, it was the throne upon which he would sit.

Fifth, Solomon would be disciplined for disobedience, but God would not remove His *lovingkindness*, as promised in verses 14-15:

> ¹⁴ *I will be his father, and he shall be my son: if he commit iniquity, I will chasten him with the rod of men, and with the stripes of the children of men;* ¹⁵ *but my lovingkindness shall not depart from him, as I took it from Saul, whom I put away before you.*

Earlier, God did remove His lovingkindness from King Saul because of disobedience. But the promise is made that although Solomon may disobey and require God's discipline, God's lovingkindness will never depart from him. The word *lovingkindness* emphasized covenant loyalty. Solomon did fall into idolatry, the worst sin possible in Scripture. The sin of Saul was not as great as the sin of Solomon. Yet, the kingdom was taken away from the House of Saul, but not the house of David. This shows the nature of an unconditional covenant. Solomon was under such a covenant, but Saul was not.

Sixth, the Messiah will come from the seed of David, as promised in I Chronicles 17:11: *And it shall come to pass, when your days are fulfilled that you must go to be with your fathers, that I will set up your seed after you, who shall be of your sons; and I will establish his kingdom.* The emphasis in the II Samuel passage is on Solomon, but in the I Chronicles passage, it is on the Messiah. Here, God is not speaking of one of David's own sons to be established upon the throne *forever*, but the seed of one of his sons coming many years later.

Seventh, the Messiah and His *throne, house,* and *kingdom* will be established *forever* (I Chronicles 17:12-15):

> [12] *He shall build me a house, and I will establish his throne forever.* [13] *I will be his father, and he shall be my son: and I will not take my lovingkindness away from him, as I took it from him that was before you;* [14] *but I will settle him in my house and in my kingdom forever; and his throne shall be established forever.* [15] *According to all these words, and according to all this vision, so did Nathan speak unto David.*

In this passage, it is the Messiah who is established upon David's throne. Clearly, the emphasis in the I Chronicles passage is not on Solomon, but on the Messiah. That is why this passage does not mention the possibility of sin as the II Samuel passage does, for, in the case of the Messiah, no sin would be possible. The Messiah, as well as His *throne*, His *house*, and His *kingdom* are to be established *forever*.

To summarize the Davidic Covenant, God promised David four eternal things: an eternal house or dynasty, an eternal throne, an eternal kingdom, and an eternal descendant. The eternality of the house, throne, and kingdom is guaranteed because the seed of David culminates in One who is Himself eternal: the Messianic God-Man.

3. The Importance of the Covenant

The unique importance of the Davidic Covenant is that it amplifies the Seed aspect of the Abrahamic Covenant. According to the Abrahamic Covenant, the Messiah was to be of the seed of Abraham. This merely stated that He was to be a Jew and could be of any of the twelve tribes. Later, in the time of Jacob, the seed aspect was limited to a member of the tribe of Judah only (Gen. 49:10). Now the Messianic seed aspect is further narrowed to one family within the tribe of Judah, the family of David.

Thus there has been a gradual narrowing of the Seed. According to the Adamic Covenant, the Messiah must be of the seed of the woman, but this meant He could come from any part of humanity. According to the Abrahamic Covenant, He had to come out of Jewish humanity, which meant He could come out of any tribe of Israel. With the confirmation of this covenant, through Jacob's twelve sons, He now had to come out of the tribe of Judah, but this permits Him to come from any family of Judah. With the Davidic Covenant, the Messiah had to come from the seed of David. It will be narrowed one step further in Jeremiah 22:24-30, which shows that the Messiah had to come from the house of David, but apart from Jeconiah.

4. The Confirmation of the Covenant

The Davidic Covenant is reconfirmed in several passages: II Samuel 23:1-5; Psalm 89:1-52; Isaiah 9:6-7; Jeremiah 23:5-6; 30:8-9; 33:14-17, 19-26; Ezekiel 37:24-25; Hosea 3:4-5; Amos 9:11; Luke 1:30-35, 68-70; Acts 15:14-18.

5. Present Status

This Covenant is also an unconditional covenant, and as such, it is still very much in effect today.

J. THE NEW COVENANT

A number of other passages speak of or relate to the New Covenant and many of these will be referenced below. But the foundational passage is Jeremiah 31:31-34.

1. The Participants in the Covenant

This covenant is made between God and Israel, and it receives further confirmation in other passages, including Isaiah 55:3; 59:21; 61:8-9; Jeremiah 32:40; Ezekiel 16:60; 34:25-31; 37:26-28; and Romans 11:26-27.

2. The Provisions of the Covenant

From the original covenant, its various confirmations, and its inauguration in the New Testament, a total of nine provisions can be listed.

First, it is an unconditional covenant involving God and both houses of Israel (v. 31): *Behold, the days come, says Jehovah, that I will make a new covenant with the house of Israel, and with the house of Judah.* It is not made merely between Judah and God or between Israel and God, but it included both houses of Israel; hence, it includes the entire Jewish nation: the descendants of Abraham, Isaac, and Jacob. It should be noted that it is not made with the Church.

Second, it is clearly distinct from the Mosaic Covenant (v. 32): *Not according to the covenant that I made with their fathers in the day that I took them by the hand to bring them out of the land of Egypt; which my covenant they broke, although I was a husband unto them, says Jehovah.* It is not merely a further elaboration of the Mosaic Covenant, but it is ultimately to replace the Mosaic Covenant, which was now considered broken.

Third, it promises the regeneration of Israel in verse 33a: *But this is the covenant that I will make with the house of Israel after those days, says Jehovah: I will put my law in their inward parts, and in their heart will I write it; and I will be their God, and they shall be my people.*

The key aspect of this entire covenant is the blessing of salvation, which included Israel's national regeneration. This is also pointed out in Isaiah 59:21.

Fourth, there is the indwelling of the Holy Spirit, in verse 33b. This is implied here but made explicit in Ezekiel 36:27.

The reason Israel failed to keep the law under the Mosaic Covenant was that the people lacked the power to comply with the righteous standards of God. The Mosaic Law did not provide the indwelling of the Holy Spirit; that was not its purpose. But the New Covenant will do just that, and every Jew will be enabled to do the righteous work of God. This is a blessing resulting from the blessing of salvation.

Fifth, the regeneration of Israel is to be universal among all Jews, as it says in verse 34a: *They shall teach no more every man his neighbor, and every man his brother, saying, Know Jehovah; for they shall all know me, from the least of them unto the greatest of them, says Jehovah.* National salvation is to extend to every individual Jewish person, and it is to be true through succeeding generations from the time that the initial regeneration of Israel occurs. Thus, during the Kingdom, the unregenerate people will all be Gentiles; in the entire period of the Kingdom, there will be no unsaved Jews. That is the reason there will be no need for one Jew to say to another, *know the Lord*, for they shall all know Him. This is also found in Isaiah 61:9.

Sixth, there is provision for the forgiveness of sin in verse 34b: *for I will forgive their iniquity, and their sin will I remember no more.* The New Covenant will do the very thing that the Mosaic Covenant was unable to do. The Mosaic Covenant was able only to cover the sins of Israel, but the New Covenant will take them away. This is a corollary blessing to the blessing of salvation.

Seventh, Ezekiel 34:25-27 tells us that Israel will be showered with material blessings:

> ^{25} *And I will make with them a covenant of peace, and will cause evil beasts to cease out of the land; and they shall dwell securely in the wilderness, and sleep in the woods.* ^{26} *And I will make them and the places round about my hill a blessing; and I will cause the shower to come down in its season; there shall be showers of blessing.* ^{27} *And the tree of the field shall yield its fruit, and the earth shall yield its increase, and they shall be secure in their land; and they shall know that I am Jehovah, when I have broken the bars of their yoke, and have delivered them out of the hand of those that made bondmen of them.*

The Mosaic Law did provide material blessings for obedience, but for the most part, Israel was in disobedience because of her failure to keep the law. However, such failure will not exist under the New Covenant. Along with Israel's regeneration and empowerment to keep the law, the Lord will give material blessings. Isaiah 61:8 and Jeremiah 32:41 also make this point.

Eighth, the Sanctuary will be rebuilt, according to Ezekiel 37:26-28:

> ^{26} *Moreover I will make a covenant of peace with them; it shall be an everlasting covenant with them; and I will place them, and multiply them, and will set my sanctuary in the midst of them forevermore.* ^{27} *My tabernacle also shall be with them; and I will be their God, and they shall be my people.* ^{28} *And the nations shall know that I am Jehovah that sanctifies Israel, when my sanctuary shall be in the midst of them for evermore.*

The Mosaic Covenant provided for the building of the Tabernacle. The Davidic Covenant provided for the building of the First Temple by Solomon and the Second Temple by Zerubbabel. The New Covenant will provide for the building of the Messianic or Millennial Temple. This Temple will be a continual reminder to Israel of all that God has done.

Ninth, just as the Mosaic Covenant contained the Law of Moses, the New Covenant contains the Law of the Messiah, in Romans 8:2 and Galatians 6:2. The Romans passage reads: *For the law of the Spirit of life in Messiah Yeshua made me free from the law of sin and death.* The Galatians passage reads: *Bear ye one another's burdens, and so fulfill the law of Messiah.*

Like the Law of Moses, the Law of the Messiah contains many individual commandments that are applicable to the New Testament believer. These commandments were given by Yeshua directly through His apostles. A simple comparison of the details will show that it is not and cannot be the same as the Law of Moses. Four observations are worth noting. First, many commandments are the same as those of the Law of Moses. For example, nine of the Ten Commandments are also in the Law of the Messiah. But second, many are different from the Law of Moses. For example, there is no Sabbath law now (Rom. 14:5; Col. 2:16) and no dietary code (Mk. 7:19; Rom. 14:20). Third, the Law of the Messiah intensifies some commandments in the Law of Moses. For example, the Law of Moses said in Leviticus 19:18: love your neighbor as yourself; this made man the standard. The Law of the Messiah said in John 15:12: love one another, even as I have loved you; this makes the Messiah the standard in that He loved man enough to die for him. Fourth, the Law of the Messiah provides a new motivation. For example, the Law of Moses was based on the conditional Mosaic Covenant, and so the motivation was: "Do, in order to be blessed." The Law of the Messiah is based on the unconditional New Covenant, and so the motivation is: "You have been and are blessed, therefore, do."

The reason there is so much confusion over the relationship of the Law of Moses and the Law of the Messiah is that many commandments are similar to those found in the Mosaic Law, and many have concluded that certain sections of the law have therefore been retained. It has already been shown that this cannot be the case, and the explanation for the sameness of the commandments is to be found elsewhere.

This explanation can best be understood if it is realized that there are a number of law codes in the Bible, such as the Edenic Code, Adamic Code, Noahic Code, Mosaic Code, New or Messianic Code, and Kingdom Code. A new code may contain some of the same commandments of the previous code, but this does not mean that the previous code is still in effect. While certain of the commandments of the Adamic Code were also found in the Edenic Code, it did not mean that the Edenic Code was still partially in force; it ceased to function with the fall of Man. The same is true when we compare the Law of the Messiah with the Law of Moses. There are many similar commandments. For example, nine of the Ten Commandments are to be found in the Law of the Messiah, but this does not mean that the Law of Moses is still in force. The Law of Moses has been rendered inoperative, and believers are now under the Law of the Messiah. There are many different commandments. For example, under the Law of Moses, a believer would not be permitted to eat pork, but under the Law of the Messiah, he may. There are many similar commandments, but they are nonetheless in two separate systems. If we do not kill or steal today, it is not because of the Law of Moses but because of the Law of the Messiah. On the other hand, if someone steals, he is not guilty of breaking the Law of Moses, but of breaking the Law of the Messiah. The present obligation to obey the Law of the Messiah is due to the present outworking of the New Covenant.

3. The Importance of the Covenant

The importance of the New Covenant is that it amplifies the blessing aspect of the Abrahamic Covenant, especially in relation to salvation. It finally shows how the spiritual blessings of the Jewish covenants extend to the Gentiles.

4. The Relationship of the Church to the New Covenant

It is at this point that some confusion has arisen as to the relationship of the Church to the New Covenant. According to Jeremiah, the covenant is made with Israel, not with the Church. Nevertheless, a number of Scriptures connect the New Covenant with the Church (Mat. 26:28; Mk. 14:24; Lk. 22:14-20; I Cor. 11:25; II Cor. 3:6; Heb. 7:22; 8:6-13; 9:15; 10:16, 29; 12:24; 13:20).

The most popular solution in Church history has been the theology of replacement or transference, which teaches that the Church has replaced Israel in its covenantal standing. Thus, the covenant promises are now being fulfilled in, by, and through the Church. It is obvious, however, that they are not being fulfilled literally, and so replacement theologians teach that the intent was for the promises to be fulfilled spiritually. But this solution requires an allegorical interpretation of the covenants and requires the ignoring of all the details such as the land promises.

Those who accept a literal approach to the covenants have rightly rejected this view and have offered two other solutions. Some writers teach that there are two new covenants, one made with the Church and one made with Israel. This view is not supported by the teachings of Scripture. Furthermore, passages that are quoted as referring to the New Covenant actually quote the New Covenant of Jeremiah which is clearly stated to be made with Israel. Others have said that there is only one New Covenant, but that it has two aspects, one relating to Israel and one relating to the Church. Yet, nothing in the New Covenant seems to teach that there are two completely different aspects. Furthermore, even those who hold this view are unable to say which aspect relates to the Church and which relates to Israel.

Actually, the solution is not so difficult, for it is clearly explained in two passages. The first is Ephesians 2:11-16:

> [11] *Wherefore remember, that once ye, the Gentiles in the flesh, who are called Uncircumcision by that which is called Circumcision, in the flesh, made by hands;* [12] *that ye were at that time separate from Messiah, alienated from the commonwealth of Israel, and strangers from the covenants of the promise, having no hope and without God in the world.* [13] *But now in Messiah Yeshua ye that once were far off are made nigh in the blood of Messiah.* [14] *For he is our peace, who made both one, and broke down the middle wall of partition,* [15] *having abolished in his flesh the enmity, even the law of commandments contained in ordinances; that he might create in himself of the two one new man, so making peace;* [16] *and might reconcile them both in one body unto God through the cross, having slain the enmity thereby:* . . .

The second passage is Ephesians 3:5-6:

> [5] *which in other generations was not made known unto the sons of men, as it has now been revealed unto his holy apostles and prophets in the Spirit;* [6] *to wit, that the Gentiles are fellow-heirs, and fellow-members of the body, and fellow-partakers of the promise in Messiah Yeshua through the gospel,* . . .

This could be called the "partaker view." The point of these passages is that God made four unconditional covenants with Israel: the Abrahamic Covenant, the Land Covenant, the Davidic Covenant, and the New Covenant. God's blessings, both physical and spiritual, are mediated by means of these four covenants. However, there is also a fifth covenant, the conditional Mosaic Covenant. This was *the middle wall of partition*. Essentially, it kept the Gentiles from enjoying the spiritual blessings of the four unconditional covenants. For a Gentile to begin receiving the blessings of the unconditional covenants, he had to totally submit to the Mosaic Law, undergo circumcision, take upon himself the obligations of the law, and, for all practical purposes, live as a son of Abraham. Gentiles-as-Gentiles were not able to enjoy the spiritual blessings of the Jewish covenants; hence, they were strangers from *the commonwealth of Israel*. However, when the Messiah died, the Mosaic Law, *the middle wall of partition*, was broken down. Now, by faith, Gentiles-as-Gentiles can enjoy the spiritual blessings of the four unconditional covenants. That is why Gentiles today are partakers of Jewish spiritual blessings, not "takers-over."

The concept of partaking is also found in Romans 11:17: *But if some of the branches were broken off, and you, being a wild olive, were grafted in among them, and did become partaker with them of the root of the fatness of the olive tree; . . .* The olive tree represents the place of spiritual blessings of the Jewish Covenants. Two types of branches are partaking of the blessings: the natural branches, which are the Jewish believers; and the wild olive branches, which are the Gentile believers.

However, the olive tree itself still belongs to Israel according to verse 24:

For if you were cut out of that which is by nature a wild olive tree, and were grafted contrary to nature into a good olive tree; how much more shall these, which are the natural branches, be grafted into their own olive tree?

The relationship of the Church to the New Covenant is the same as the Church's relationship to the Abrahamic Covenant, the Land Covenant, and the Davidic Covenant. The physical promises of the Abrahamic Covenant, as amplified by the Land and Davidic Covenants, were promised exclusively to Israel. However, the blessing aspect, as amplified by the New Covenant, was to include the Gentiles. The Church is enjoying the spiritual blessings of these covenants, not the material and physical benefits. The physical promises still belong to Israel and will be fulfilled exclusively with Israel, especially those involving the Land. However, the Church is now sharing all spiritual benefits. This is the Church's relationship to these four unconditional covenants between God and Israel.

The blood of the Messiah is the basis of salvation in the New Covenant, and it was shed at the cross. It ratified, signed, and sealed the New Covenant (Heb. 8:1-10:18). The provisions of the New Covenant cannot be fulfilled in, by, or through the Church, but have to be fulfilled in, by, and through Israel. It is true that the New Covenant is not now being fulfilled by Israel, but this does not mean it is therefore being fulfilled by the Church. As seen before, not all provisions of a covenant have to go into effect immediately. The Church is related to the New Covenant only insofar as it partakes of the spiritual benefits of the New Covenant, such as the salvation benefit. The Church has become a *partaker* of Jewish spiritual blessings, but the Church is not a taker-over of the Jewish covenants. Also the Church partakes of the spiritual blessings and promises, but not the material or physical blessings.

5. The Gentile Obligation

The fact that Gentile believers have become partakers of Jewish spiritual blessings places an obligation on them, according to Romans 15:25-27:

> ^{25} but now, I say, I go unto Jerusalem, ministering unto the saints. ^{26} For it has been the good pleasure of Macedonia and Achaia to make a certain contribution for the poor among the saints that are at Jerusalem. ^{27} Yea, it has been their good pleasure; and their debtors they are. For if the Gentiles have been made partakers of their spiritual things, they owe it to them to minister unto them in carnal things.

As Paul came close to ending his letter to the Romans, he spelled out his immediate plans. In verse 25, he explained why he could not come to them immediately. While he had expressed a long-term desire to go to Rome in chapter one, his desire was subject to his duty, which was to collect an offering and take it to the Jewish believers in Jerusalem. This special offering is spoken of elsewhere—in I Corinthians 16:1-4 and II Corinthians 8-9. In verse 26, Paul named the contributors and the recipients of the offering. The Gentile believers of Macedonia and Achaia had given the money, which was specifically for the poor Jewish believers of Jerusalem in the land of Israel. In verse 27, Paul taught Gentile indebtedness to the Jews. He clearly stated that Gentiles are debtors to the Jews and then gave the reason for this: Gentiles have become *fellow-partakers* of Jewish spiritual blessings. Earlier, in Romans 11, Paul taught that the Gentiles have become partakers of spiritual blessings, but these are Jewish spiritual blessings that are mediated through the Jewish covenants. The very fact that Gentiles have been made *partakers* of Jewish spiritual blessings has put them into debt to the Jews. According to this verse, the way they pay their indebtedness to Jewish believers is to minister to them in material things.

6. Basis for a Dispensation and Present Status

In relation to the Church, then, the New Covenant is the basis of the Dispensation of Grace. In relation to Israel, it is the basis for the Dispensation of the Kingdom. The covenant is unconditional and therefore eternally in effect.

K. CONCLUSION

All spiritual blessings are for believers in the Messiah, whether they are Jews or Gentiles. And through His death on the cross for their sins, believers reap spiritual benefits that would never be theirs otherwise. The eight covenants of the Bible are very explicit in their provisions and are valuable for a proper understanding of Scripture.[40]

---

[40] Suggestion 3 on page 117

L. Questions and Study Suggestions

Question 1: Are you a Jew or Gentile? Have you considered Israel to be the chosen people of God? Will this influence the understanding of God's Word in your life as you see how God works first with mankind and then also with Israel?

Suggestion 1: On page 134, you will find a template of a chart you can use to systematize the eight covenants of the Bible. Start filling in the blanks as you go through the next paragraphs.

Question 2: Have you considered man's temptation and subsequent fall in relation to Satan? Is it logical that Satan had a domain before man was created on the sixth day? Where did God put Satan before he turned against God, and where did God put Satan after he rose up against God? What was his previous name? Reading the 'Six Abodes of Satan' (manuscript # 001) by this author will give understanding to the context of what is happening at this point in Genesis.

Question 3: Taking care to handle the Scriptures with correct rules of interpretation, can you see how attacks on Scripture can often be surrounded by and based in ignorance and error? Have you been challenged in your own heart to view Scripture as erroneous at times on subjects that you might not have studied thoroughly yet?

Question 4: After studying *The Nature of the Bible*, *The Bible and Divine Revelation*, and *The Inspiration of the Scriptures*, can you see how vast and large the scope of this writing of God is? Journal how this affects your understanding of God. How well do you think God understands you?

Question 5: Are there parts of the Adamic Covenant that have affected your life in a very real and present sense on a daily level?

Question 6: If you have studied the end times, have you ever tied the breaking of the Noahic Covenant to the judgment of fire?

Question 7: Although the chart of this study does not include this dynamic of clarification, can you see how thorough God's sovereignty is through all of time? If God is so sovereign as to tie time and covenants together for mankind, does it make sense that we can trust and worship Him daily for providing the access to know Him personally?

Suggestion 2: As the study of eight covenants continues, keep in mind that the next section of study will be the seven dispensations. To put the perspective of God's sovereignty through time with His purpose for His creation as well as giving Israel a choice to obey or disobey is critical for knowing God and understanding

Scripture as a whole. The study of dispensations that follows will further put a context to the whole of time and therefore deeply reveal the character of God to you. Journal the observations that come before you so that you can look back on your learning experience.

Suggestion 3: Take the online test for this section of the study of the Word of God found on http://ariel.org/come-and-see.htm under "The Eight Covenants of the Bible (021)," quiz.

THE EIGHT COVENANTS OF THE BIBLE				
Two Types of Covenants		The Covenants	
Conditional Covenants	Unconditional Covenants	Five were made with ___ exclusively	Two were made with _____ in general
A conditional covenant is a_____ These are_____	An unconditional covenant is a_____ These are_____	One is conditional: Four are unconditional:	
^	^	Four things should be noted concerning the nature of the unconditional covenants made with Israel: _____	
The Principle of the Timing of the Provisions A covenant can be signed, sealed, and made at a specific point of history, but_____			
NAME OF COVENANT	**PARTICIPANTS IN THE COVENANT**	**PROVISIONS OF THE COVENANT**	**THE STATUS OF THE COVENANT**
_____	_____	_____	_____

The Word of God

Chapter VI
The Dispensations of God

One key to understanding the Scriptures is to "rightly divide the Word of Truth" (II Tim. 2:15). There are a number of different ways the Bible can be divided in order to understand the parts as well as the whole. One of the ways is by means of the dispensations which are contained in the Scriptures. These dispensations are based on specific covenants so that the covenants work their way out during the dispensations and become the rule of life for a number of the dispensations.[41]

A. Definition

What is a dispensation? In dealing with this question, we are going to discuss five key areas: the etymology, Scripture usage, and definition of the word, its facets, and the mark of a dispensationalist.

1. Etymology

Studying the etymology of the word "dispensation," one is concerned with both the English and the Greek terms. The English word "dispensation" comes from the Latin term *dispensatio*, which means "the weighing out" or "the dispensing." There are three principle ideas in the English word "dispensation." It first describes the act of

---

[41] Suggestion 1 on page 142

dealing out or distributing. The second key idea is the act of administering, ordering, or managing the system by which things are administered. The third key idea is the action of dispensing some requirement.

The Latin root word is found in the Vulgate version of the Bible where it translates two different Greek terms. One of them is *oikonomia*. This is where we get the English word "ecumenical" from. But this Greek word did not refer to a movement towards unity. It is really closer to the concept of "dispensation." *Oikonomia* meant "to manage, to regulate, to administer, and to plan." The word is a compound of two separate Greek words: *oikos*, which means "a house," and *nomos*, which means "law." So it is "house/law" or "law/house." Therefore, *oikonomia* means "to divide," "to apportion," "to administer," "to manage the affairs of an inhabited house." The central idea in the word "dispensation" is the act of managing or administering the affairs of a household.

The second Greek word is *aion*, and it is often translated by the English word "world." However, a better English translation would be the word "age." This word gives a time-element to "dispensation." By itself, the word "dispensation" does not contain a time-element, as it is often misconstrued to mean. The term "dispensation" refers to an administration, a dispensing of the affairs of a household. However, when it is compounded with the Greek word *aion*, the time-element is added.

In concluding the etymology, we can say that as to content and meaning, "dispensation" means "a stewardship." As to time, it is "an age."

2. Scripture Usage of the Words

The word *oikonomia* is used twenty times in the Scriptures. In its verb form— οἰκονομέω (*oikonomeo*)—it is used only once, in Luke 16:2, where it is translated as "to be a steward or manager." The second form is the noun οἰκονόμος (*oikonomos*), which is used ten times: Luke 12:42; 16:1, 3, 8; Romans 16:23; I Corinthians 4:1-2; Galatians 4:2; Titus 1:7; I Peter 4:10. In all ten cases, it is translated as "a steward." The third form of the word is οἰκονομία (*oikonomia*), which is used nine times: Luke 16:2-4; I Corinthians 9:17; Ephesians 1:10; 3:2, 9; Colossians 1:25; I Timothy 1:4. In these nine cases, it is translated either as "a dispensation" or as "a stewardship."

From these twenty usages of the term, we can deduct two main features. The first is parabolic usage and is found in Luke 12:42 and 16:1, 3, and 8. This usage refers to the management of a household by a steward. We see two parties; one has the authority to delegate duties, and the other has the responsibility to carry them out. One is the master, and one is the steward. Furthermore, there are specific responsibilities which each must carry out, and there is accountability built in as part of the arrangement. A steward may be called upon to account for the discharge of his stewardship. In the parabolic usage, a change may be made at any time if unfaithfulness is found in an existing administration.

Second, with one exception of I Peter 4:10, the word *oikonomia* is used only by Paul. Studying these other usages, we discover six things: First, God is the One to whom men are responsible in the discharge of their stewardship. This is brought out by I Corinthians 4:1-2 and Titus 1:7. Second, faithfulness is required of those to whom a dispensational responsibility is committed. This is taught by I Corinthians 4:2, and we have an example of it in Romans 16:23. Third, a stewardship may be brought to an end at an appointed time, which is seen in Galatians 4:7. The dispensation may end because a different purpose has been introduced. It is this particular aspect of a dispensation that carries with it a time element, although the word itself does not require it. Fourth, dispensations are connected with the mysteries of God and deal with specific divine revelations. A new dispensation often came into being by virtue of new revelation. This is brought out in I Corinthians 4:1, Ephesians 3:2, and Colossians 1:25. Fifth, the terms "dispensation" and "age" are connected ideas. But they are neither exactly the same nor interchangeable. For example, the revelation of the present dispensation was hidden for ages, according to Ephesians 3:9 and Colossians 1:26. Thus, a dispensation does operate within a time period. Sixth, at least three different dispensations are mentioned by Paul. The first is in Ephesians 1:10, which talks about "the dispensation of the fullness of time," that is, the Dispensation of the Kingdom. The second is in Ephesians 3:2, where Paul speaks of "the dispensation of the grace of God." This is the present dispensation in which we live: the Dispensation of Grace. The third is in Colossians 1:25-26, where Paul speaks of a dispensation which preceded the present one, which was "the Dispensation of the Law." So Paul clearly spoke of at least three specific dispensations by name: the Dispensation of the Law, the Dispensation of Grace, and the Dispensation of the Kingdom.

3. Definition

Based upon our previous discussion on the etymology and the scriptural usages of the word, we can now derive a clear-cut definition of what a dispensation is. A dispensation "is a distinguishable economy in the outworking of God's purposes."[42]

With that definition, Ryrie brings out three ramifications based upon three key statements. First, a dispensation is an *economy*, suggesting that certain features of different dispensations may be the same or similar. A second ramification is that it is *distinguishable*, emphasizing that there are some features which are distinctive to each dispensation and which mark them off from one another. So on the one hand, certain features are the same, and on the other hand, certain features are different. The third ramification is that it involves *the outworking of God's purposes*. This means that the viewpoint of distinguishing the various dispensations is God's, not man's, and that the dispensations work their way out for God's, not man's purposes. In other words, dispensations develop from one to another only from God's side. A distinguishable economy occurs when three things fall into place: First, there is a continuation of certain ordinances which were valid until then. For example, the ordinance not to kill was valid during a previous dispensation and may be true of a new dispensation.

Second, there is an annulment of other regulations which had been valid until then. One example is the regulation under the Noahic Covenant that allowed man to eat anything he wanted. For the Jewish people, this was annulled with the Mosaic Covenant, when regulations were introduced governing what was permissible to eat and what was not.

Third, there is an introduction of fresh principles or new ordinances with new regulations, which were not valid until then. One example is the rule under the Mosaic Law to not eat pork. It became forbidden in the new dispensation, which was simply not true before the Mosaic Law was given.

As noted before, a dispensation is a distinguishable economy in the outworking of God's purposes. But adding to this definition, a dispensation is a stage in the progressive revelation of God, constituting a distinctive stewardship or rule of life. In the study of Bibliology, one learns about progressive revelation, pointing out that God did not choose to reveal everything at once, but instead gave us His revelation over a period of 1,600 years. When more revelation was given, this

---

[42] Ryrie, Charles C., *Dispensationalism* (Chicago: Moody Press, 1995), p. 23-43.

frequently involved a new dispensational stage. Any new revelation usually goes hand in hand with a continuation of certain things, an annulment of other things, and an addition of new rules, all of which requires new revelation. Thus, it can be concluded that dispensationalism is the only systematic theology that seriously deals with the issue of progressive revelation.

Now, expanding the definition from the simple to the complex, here is a more detailed definition of dispensations and dispensationalism:[43]

> Dispensationalism views the world as a household run by God, and in this household world, God is dispensing or administering its affairs according to His own will and in various stages of revelation in the process of time. These various stages mark off the different distinguishable economies in the outworking of God's total purpose. These economies are the dispensations. The understanding of God's different economies is essential to a proper interpretation of His revelation within these various economies.

It is essential that one understands this more detailed definition if he is going to grasp all that is involved in dispensationalism. This definition and understanding is going to prove true and be essential to understanding all realms of systematic theology.

There is one last thing in the area of definition, and that is the distinction of viewpoints. From God's viewpoint, a dispensation is an economy. But from man's viewpoint a dispensation is a responsibility, because in each new economy God gives new revelation that requires a reaction from man. Man is responsible for responding to this new revelation correctly. The distinction of viewpoint is that from God's side, it is an economy where He is dispensing the affairs of His household-world in keeping with His own will and purpose. But from man's side, this thing that God is dispensing carries responsibilities to which man must respond. There is further the viewpoint of progressive revelation, where a dispensation is a stage in its progress. What starts off a new dispensation and what

---

[43] Ryrie, Charles C., *Dispensationalism* (Chicago: Moody Press, 1995), p. 23-43.

ends a previous one is invariably over the issue of what God has chosen to reveal only at a specific point in time.

In summarizing the distinction of viewpoints, we can say that with God, a dispensation is an economy, while with man, it is a responsibility. In regards to progressive revelation, a dispensation is a stage in it.[44]

4. The Facets of a Dispensation

There are seven specific elements or facets involved in each dispensation.
1) Each dispensation has one or more names which somehow show what the basic rule of life was for that particular dispensation.
2) Each dispensation has a chief person to whom special revelation is given.
3) Each dispensation provides a responsibility to man because each dispensation begins with new revelation that requires a human response.
4) There is a specific test.
5) Following the test is a specific failure.
6) There is a judgment that brings the dispensation to an end.
7) Each dispensation has something that characterizes divine grace.[45]

5. The Mark of a Dispensationalist[46]

What is it that finally determines who is and who is not a dispensationalist? What is the mark of a dispensationalist? We will answer this question in three ways.

a. What it is not

What does **not** indicate that one is a dispensationalist? There are three negatives. First, it is not a recognition that dispensations exist, because even non-dispensationalists and anti-dispensationalists believe in at least two dispensations: the Old and the New Testament dispensations. The fact that someone recognizes that dispensations exist does not mean that he is a dispensationalist.

---

[44] Question 1 on page 142

[45] Suggestion 2 on page 142

[46] This point is largely a paraphrase of Ryrie's *Dispensationalism*.

Second, it does not relate to the number of dispensations. While most dispensationalists believe in seven dispensations, there are some who hold to less or more than seven. To be a dispensationalist you have to believe in a minimum of three dispensations: the Old Testament dispensation, the New Testament dispensation, and a future millennial dispensation.

Third, it is not premillennialism or even pretribulationalism that makes one a dispensationalist. Just because one believes in a literal kingdom on this earth and is premillennial, that does not make him a dispensationalist. There are premillennialists who are non-dispensational and some who are even anti-dispensational. And there are premillennialists who are also pretribulationalists, but who are non-dispensational and even anti-dispensational.

b. What it is

The question therefore arises: On what basis does one class himself as a dispensationalist? Here again, three things can be noted.

First, he would hold to a consistent, plain hermeneutic, rather than over-spiritualizing or allegorizing the text. This is a literal, normal, or plain interpretation of Scripture. A dispensationalist takes the Bible literally, as it reads, and does not attempt to spiritualize away its plain meaning or read it as an allegory for something else. The stress of this position is on consistency. All believers of all persuasions take at least some parts of the Bible literally, but a dispensationalist will consistently follow this golden rule of interpretation. It should be noted that this does not mean that dispensationalists do not recognize figures of speech or fail to recognize that the Bible does use symbolic language. But where a symbol is used, it is explained either in the immediate context or elsewhere in the Bible, and the explanation comes through the literal interpretation of those explanations. So a dispensationalist is one who uses a consistent, literal hermeneutic when interpreting the Scriptures.

The second mark of a dispensationalist is that he makes a consistent distinction between Israel and the Church. It is this second mark which is the most fundamental test. The major system of theology that contradicts dispensationalism is covenant theology, which mars the distinction between Israel and the Church. A dispensationalist will say that Israel is always Israel and the Church is always the Church. Never is the Church called Israel, and never is Israel called the Church. This greatly changes how one sees and interprets Scripture, which is why this distinction between Israel and the Church is the most essential test of a true dispensationalist.

The third mark of a dispensationalist is how he sees the ultimate purpose of God. In dispensationalism, the ultimate purpose of God is doxological, meaning it is His own glory. So the ultimate purpose of God is to bring about His own glorification, and for the dispensationalist, this is the unifying theme of the whole Bible. This doxological unifying theme throughout Scripture is attained by God through many means. Covenant theologians, who oppose dispensationalism, believe that salvation is the one and only purpose of God and that salvation is the unifying theme of all Scripture. But the dispensationalist believes the plan of salvation is only one means whereby He attains the goal of His glory, and some of the other means have nothing to do with salvation. God's plan for the angels, for example, does not involve salvation, because God did not provide salvation for fallen angels. So for the dispensationalist, God's plan of salvation is only one of several programs by which He brings about His own glory.

c. Conclusion

In conclusion, we can say this: The essence of dispensationalism is the distinction between Israel and the Church, and this distinction grows out of the dispensationalist's consistent employment of the normal, plain, literal interpretation of Scripture. This reflects an understanding of the basic, key purpose of God in all of His dealings with mankind as being that of glorifying Himself through salvation and many other purposes as well. Thus, the key principle is once again progressive revelation.

B. THE DISPENSATIONS

Among dispensationalists, the general consensus is that there are seven dispensations in Scripture. In this study, each dispensation will be discussed individually.

1. The Dispensation of Innocence or Freedom: Genesis 1:28-3:8

a. The Names

The first dispensation is given two names: the Dispensation of Innocence or the Dispensation of Freedom. The names are used to emphasize different aspects of this dispensation. The first name emphasizes the fact that Adam and Eve were innocent of any sin or sin-nature at this time. Theologically, their state is called "unconfirmed creaturely holiness" in that they were created holy. But the holiness of Adam and Eve had not yet been confirmed because they had not yet been tested as to whether they would stay true to the Word of God. The second name emphasizes their freedom from sin; they were not slaves to sin. While sin was already in existence in the angelic realm, there was no sin in the human realm.

b. The Chief Person

The key person for the first dispensation was Adam. God revealed His will, divine economy, and divine administration through Adam, who thus became the representative head of the human race.

c. Man's Responsibility

Man's responsibility was to the Edenic Covenant, the covenant that God had made with Adam and Eve in the Garden of Eden (Gen. 1:28-30; 2:15-17). The basic content of the Edenic Covenant contained two aspects: responsibility to the earth and responsibility to the Garden of Eden. Concerning the earth, they were responsible to subdue it, to replenish it, to multiply on the earth, and to take control of it in general. Concerning the garden, they were responsible to till it.

d. Man's Specific Test

The specific test concerned *the tree of the knowledge of good and evil* (Gen. 2:17). This was a test to see if Adam and Eve would obey the most minimal demand of the divine will. They had absolute authority over the entire planet. As far as the Garden of Eden itself was concerned, they had absolute authority over it and had the right to eat of every single tree in the garden, including *the tree of life*. So the test was very minimal.

If Adam and Eve had passed the test, their state would have changed from unconfirmed creaturely holiness to confirmed creaturely holiness. This means that they would have passed from the ability to sin to the ability not to sin; they would no longer have the ability to sin after their holiness was confirmed. This was the same kind of test that all of the angels underwent when they were first created. All angels were created in unconfirmed creaturely holiness. Then came the test. Satan was the first to fail, and he was followed by one-third of the entire angelic host, who are now totally corrupt. Two-thirds of the angels did pass the test, changing their state from unconfirmed creaturely holiness to confirmed creaturely holiness. Now they are no longer able to sin whatsoever.

The same thing would have been true for Adam and Eve. Had they passed this test, they would have been confirmed in creaturely holiness just as the good angels and would not have been able to sin anymore.

e. Man's Failure

Unfortunately, Adam and Eve did fail the test (Gen. 3:1-8). They ate of the very tree from which they were forbidden to eat. As a result, their creaturely holiness was not confirmed. Just as the fallen angels, they, too, were corrupted and became totally depraved in their nature. Total depravity means that sin had touched every part of their being and every area of their human lives.

f. Man's Judgment

The judgment in this dispensation was expulsion from the garden and the curse upon the earth (Gen. 3:9-19). The expulsion from the garden meant they were now expelled to a place outside the garden, and the tremendous environment that they had within the garden was no longer available to them. They would no longer be able to eat freely from every tree found in the garden, nor would they be able to eat from *the tree of life*.

Instead of having an easy working relationship with the ground, the toilsome aspect of labor was added. Adam would now have to work the earth by the sweat of his brow in order to be able to eat. Furthermore, the curse meant the earth would no longer be his friend, but his enemy. As Adam would try to produce things from the earth, he would have a continual war with *thorns* and *thistles*.

g. God's Display of Grace

The display of God's grace is seen in that at the same time as the expulsion from the garden and the cursing of the earth took place, God also promised a Redeemer. In Genesis 3:15, God promised that someday Messiah would come who would do two things: First, He would defeat the enemy of man, Satan, who brought about the curse, the expulsion, and the fall of man through his temptation. And second, He would be the One who would conquer the curse and have the curse removed. Physical death, which was a result of the fall of man, would be overcome by the resurrection of that Last Adam and by the ultimate resurrection of all people.

2. The Dispensation of Conscience or Self-Determination: Genesis 3:9-8:14

a. The Names

The second dispensation also has two names: the Dispensation of Conscience or the Dispensation of Self-Determination. The first name emphasizes the principle by which God dispensed His economy; conscience was the way God governed mankind in this dispensation. The name comes from Romans 2:15, which states that God dealt with men for a period of time on the basis of their conscience until, finally, their conscience became so defiled and seared that it was no longer possible to continue governing God's economy in the world in this way.

The second name emphasizes the other side of the coin of conscience; man was given the freedom to follow the dictates of his conscience. His obligation was to follow through with what his conscience demanded. If he followed his conscience, his self-determination would have led to holiness; but if he did not follow his conscience, or if his conscience was defiled, blackened, darkened, or seared, then his self-determination would go in the opposite direction.

b. The Chief Person

The chief person was the same as in the previous one, Adam. Adam received some new revelation that spelled out the principles and requirements of this new dispensation. Once again, he served as the representative head of all humanity.

c. Man's Responsibility

Man's responsibility was obedience to the Adamic Covenant, found in Genesis 3. Among the requirements of the Adamic Covenant were: the responsibility of the wife to be in subjection to her husband; the working of the land in toil and sweat of the brow; the concept of physical death.

The key element in this responsibility was faith in the promised Redeemer. Contained within the scope of this covenant was the promise of verse 15, in which God told Satan: *I will put enmity between you and the woman, and between your seed and her seed: He shall bruise your head, and you shall bruise his heel.* This verse promised that a time was coming when a human descendant of the same woman that Satan had tempted, bringing about the fall of man, would someday conquer Satan and crush his head.

The promise was that the Messiah would be after the Seed of the woman. As we saw in the previous chapter, this goes contrary to the normal biblical pattern.

Normally, a man's line was traced through the genealogy of the father, not the mother. It was always through the seed of the male, not the seed of the female. That is why all the genealogies in Scripture always contain the male line, and females are seldom mentioned in them. In the case of the Messiah, however, it was going to be different. The Messiah would be reckoned after the Seed of the woman, not the man.

Genesis 3:15 does not explain why that would have to be so. In fact, this is not explained until Isaiah 7:14, where God stated that the Messiah would be born of a virgin. The clear reason why the Messiah would have to be reckoned after the *seed of the woman* was that He would not have a human father.

Man's responsibility was to believe the promise, that someday the Seed of the woman, the Messiah, would come and redeem them from *the prince of this world*, Satan. Although in the previous dispensation and covenant, God gave the authority over this earth to man, when Adam fell, Satan usurped the authority from man. Therefore, even in the New Testament, Satan is called *the prince of this world* (Jn. 12:31) and *the god of this age* (II Cor. 4:4).

d. Man's Specific Test

The specific test was twofold: first, man's obedience was to the dictates of conscience in the knowledge of good and evil. And second, when there was failure, they were to offer a proper and acceptable blood sacrifice. The principle of blood was introduced early; in fact, before Adam and Eve were expelled from the garden. In Genesis 3:21, God made them coats of animal skin to cover their nakedness. This principle was understood because the acceptable sacrifice brought by Abel in Genesis 4:4 was a blood sacrifice.

e. Man's Failure

Failure was seen as early as the case of Cain in Genesis 4:3. Cain failed to bring a proper blood sacrifice and thought he could come to God on his own terms rather than on the terms that God had ordained. In verse eight, failure was seen in the first act of murder when Cain murdered his brother Abel.

But failure is also seen in Genesis 6:5, which speaks of open violence, corruption, widespread evil, and continuous evil desire in the heart and the purpose of man.

f. Man's Judgment

The judgment in this dispensation was the worldwide flood (Gen. 6:6-7:23); to bring humanity to an end with the exception of one family. With the worldwide flood, this dispensation came to an end. Humanity had become evil to the point that they could no longer follow their conscience, because their conscience was so darkened and degenerate that it was no longer a reliable guide whatsoever.

g. God's Display of Grace

Displays of God's grace are seen in that man did have knowledge of God's will; they knew that God provided a blood atonement to deal with the problem of sin. The element of grace in this dispensation is seen in the salvation of Enoch (Gen. 5:18-23). It was also seen in the rescue of Noah and his family. All of these people found grace in the eyes of the Lord.

3. The Dispensation of Civil Government: Genesis 8:15-11:32

a. The Names

The name Civil Government comes from one of the provisions of the Noahic Covenant that whoever sheds man's blood, by a man must his blood be shed. So now, judicial authority is given to man over life and death. The concept of ruling and having power to execute or not to execute contains within it the concepts of human government. This principle is in Genesis 9:6: *Whoso sheds man's blood, by man shall his blood be shed.* So man is given the authority to execute the murderer, and this carries with it the concept of rule, authority, and government. One of the main functions of human government is to restrain lawlessness. The previous dispensation showed that conscience could not restrain lawlessness.

b. The Chief Person

The chief person in this dispensation was Noah. He received new and specific divine revelation that told him exactly how the divine economy in this dispensation of God would be run. Like Adam, Noah stood as the representative head of the human race. Now, all humanity descended not only from Adam, but also from Noah.

c. Man's Responsibility

Human responsibility was obedience to the Noahic Covenant of Genesis 9. Contained within the scope of the Noahic Covenant was that man must replenish and fill the earth in light of the destruction of humanity by the Flood (vv. 1, 7).

No dietary limitations whatsoever were placed upon man under the Noahic Covenant (vv. 3-5). Man was to be vegetarian in the two preceding dispensations.

From this point on, however, man was allowed to go beyond the limit of vegetables and eat any kind of meat he chose.

Furthermore, the Noahic Covenant was to establish human government, through which God was going to dispense or govern His economy. Man was responsible to obey human government, which would have the authority to enforce its rules and regulations to the point of execution (vv. 5-6).

The rainbow was given as a sign or token of the Noahic Covenant, thereby promising that God would never again destroy the earth with a flood (vv. 12-17).

d. Man's Specific Test

The specific test involved two elements: first, man was to rule justly; and second, humanity was to spread throughout the world. They were not to be under only one government in one place; God demanded that they disperse all over the earth.

e. Man's Failure

The failure is seen in what men tried to achieve in Genesis 11. Instead of spreading out as God had commanded them to do, they tried to stay together, using the Tower of Babel as a literal and symbolic center. The Tower of Babel was to reach "unto heaven." It was supposed to be high enough to give good visibility for the study of the stars. This was not for the sake of astronomy, but for the sake of astrology. The study of astrology meant a repudiation of God's control as the ultimate and only Creator. Astrology was a repudiation of the worship of the One God, and man began to move into polytheism and all kinds of other sins as well. That was the physical purpose of the Tower of Babel.

Behind all these things lay demonism and that is where the failure was clearly seen. The symbolic purpose of the tower was to deliberately disobey God's command to spread all over the world. It was to serve as a center of attraction to keep humanity together. Basically, their intent was not to move outside of the Babylonian area, which lies between the Euphrates and the Tigris rivers.

Also instead of using government properly, they tried to build empires as the story of Nimrod points out in Genesis 10:8-14. Nimrod was a mighty hunter, but he was also the first empire-builder. Instead of seeing each kingdom as being independent, he tried to unify them under his authority and into one empire.

f. Man's Judgment

As a result of man's attempt to rebel against God's commands and authority, God sent a judgment: the confusion of tongues (Gen. 11:6-8). One of the key elements of societies is the common language. Once there is a differentiation of language, the consequence usually is war.

For instance, the reason Germans tend to stay together in Germany is because the German language keeps them together. The same thing is true for other countries as well. When there is a difference in language within one country, it often leads to civil war, as in the various states of Europe where one part of a nation spoke one language and another part spoke a different language. With the lack of a common language, there is turmoil, confusion, conflict, and war. By causing the confusion of tongues, God accomplished a forced dispersion.

This does not mean that every human being at that point spoke a different language altogether. What might have happened is something like this: five people found that they were able to communicate by speaking the same language so they migrated somewhere to separate themselves from the others that they could not understand. As a result, they would move to a certain part of the world and speak such and such language. On the other hand, ten or fifteen other people found themselves speaking the same language, and they, too, moved to another part of the world to separate themselves from those they could not understand, establish their own language-group and, therefore, their own unique nationality. That is the way God accomplished His original intent: man was to spread throughout the entire world and replenish it.

g. God's Display of Grace

Grace was displayed in the way God preserved the messianic line after the Flood (vv. 10-32). It is made up of the people whose names are listed after the Tower of Babel incident. These names in Genesis 11 trace the genealogy of Noah and Shem all the way down to Abraham, with whom God will bring about the next dispensation. They were followers of the one true God during this period.

God maintained the Seed-line. The promise He made concerning the Seed of the woman continued to be preserved in spite of the Flood and in spite of the Tower of Babel. God preserved the unique Seed-line through which the promise was indeed going to be fulfilled.

4. The Dispensation of Promise or Patriarchal Rule: Genesis 12:1 to Exodus 18:27

a. The Names

This dispensation is also given two names: the Dispensation of Promise and the Dispensation of Patriarchal Rule. The more common name is the first one, which emphasizes the revelational aspect in that God was revealing Himself by making a specific series of promises. The name is derived from four passages in the New Testament: Romans 4:1-25; Galatians 3:15-19; Hebrews 6:13-15; and 11:9. In all four of these passages, the key thing to notice is the emphasis on the concept of promise in relation to Abraham.

The second name emphasizes the governmental aspect. God was applying His governance and His will in this dispensation by means of His Patriarchs: Abraham, Isaac, and Jacob.

b. The Chief Person

The key person for this dispensation is Abraham. Abraham stands as the head of this new age, and new divine revelation is given to him, which then becomes the basis of a new dispensation. He also stands as the representative head of the Jewish nation.

c. Man's Responsibility

The responsibility in this dispensation was based on the Abrahamic Covenant: the responsibility to believe the promises of God. Even though the promises may not have been realized, yet the people were to believe the promises of God. Abraham, of course, carried out this responsibility in Genesis 15:6: *And he believed in Jehovah; and he reckoned it to him for righteousness.*

d. Man's Specific Test

The specific test was to stay in the land where God had brought them, but they were to be distinct and separated from the Canaanites.

e. Man's Failure

Man's failure is seen in the tendency to leave the land. For example, Abraham left the land in Genesis 12 and got himself into a lot of trouble. Isaac was contemplating leaving the land in Genesis 26, but God warned him against doing so. Only, Jacob left the land with God's blessing, but that led to Egyptian slavery.

Failure was also seen on the part of the Israelites when they began relationships with the Canaanites by intermarrying and entering business partnerships. Abraham sent his servant back to his homeland to find a wife for Isaac. Esau intermarried with the Canaanites, but Isaac sent Jacob to that same homeland to find a wife. When Jacob came back to the Land with twelve sons, those sons began intermarrying with the Canaanites. One key passage in Genesis illustrates this. In chapter 38, the focus is on the key son, Judah, because he was the one who will produce the messianic line. Judah had business relationships and partnerships with Canaanites. He married a Canaanite, his sons married Canaanites, and he finally degenerated into the immorality of the Canaanites.

f. Man's Judgment

Ultimately, the judgment for failure was the Egyptian bondage. The sojourn to Egypt was by divine command, and God prepared the way to Egypt to separate the chosen family from the Canaanites. But this was followed by the Egyptian bondage, which preserved the nation from any further interbreeding.

g. God's Display of Grace

The facet of grace was seen in the preservation of Israel both ethnically and religiously. Israel was preserved whether they were in the Land or outside the Land. God continued to preserve the Seed of the woman, now also to be the Seed of Abraham, Isaac, and Jacob.

5. The Dispensation of Law: Exodus 19:1 to Acts 1:26

a. The Name

This dispensation gets its name from the fact that God's economy was being dispensed through the Law of Moses that contained a total of 613 specific commandments.

This dispensation covers a period of time from the giving of the law in Exodus 19:1 through Acts 1:26. The Dispensation of Law covered the entire span of time from Exodus 19:1 throughout the rest of the Old Testament, the intertestamental period, and gospel history until Acts 1:26, when the dispensation finally changed.

b. The Chief Person

The key person was Moses. It was Moses to whom God gave a lot of revelation on which this dispensation was based.

c. Man's Responsibility

Man was responsible to the Mosaic Covenant, which involved two major areas. First, they were responsible to obey the 613 commandments of the Law of Moses.

Second, they were to obey the prophets whom God would send to further elaborate on the law by defining it, giving meaning to it, and explaining it.

d. Man's Specific Test

The specific test involved two major things. First, man was responsible to keep the entire law, with all of its 613 commandments. The breaking of only one of these commandments meant to incur guilt for breaking them all (Jas. 2:10).

The second part of the test was to accept and believe the Prophet who would arise, because He would be was going to be the *prophet like unto Moses* (Deut. 18:15-18).

e. Man's Failure

Man failed in both aspects of the test. First, they failed to keep the law in its entirety (Rom. 10:1-3). In fact, not only did they fail to keep the law, they tried to get around the law by establishing their own righteousness. They developed their own codex and claimed that because they obeyed their laws, they did not have to obey the laws of God.

Second, they failed to obey the prophets. The key verses on this are II Chronicles 36:14-16:

> [14] *Moreover all the chiefs of the priests, and the people, trespassed very greatly after all the abominations of the nations; and they polluted the house of Jehovah which he had hallowed in Jerusalem.* [15] *And Jehovah, the God of their fathers, sent to them by his messengers, rising up early and sending, because he had compassion on his people, and on his dwelling-place:* [16] *but they mocked the messengers of God, and despised his words, and scoffed at his prophets, until the wrath of Jehovah arose against his people, till there was no remedy.*

Verse 14 describes their idolatry. Verse 15 says that God sends the prophets, but verse 16 shows their rejection of His words and their consistent disobedience to

His prophets *till there was no remedy*. Consequently, they also failed to accept the Messiah (Mat. 23:1-39). *Yeshua* denounced the leadership of Israel of that day, the Scribes and Pharisees, not only because they rejected His messianic claims, but also because they were leading the nation to the reject those same messianic claims.

f. Man's Judgment

Several judgments can fall within a dispensation, followed by a climactic one. Two key judgments within this dispensation were the Assyrian Captivity of the northern kingdom, Israel, and the Babylonian Captivity of the southern kingdom, Judah. The climactic judgment of this dispensation came in A.D. 70 and involved two things: first, the destruction of Jerusalem and the Temple; and second, the worldwide forced dispersion of the Jewish people as they were exiled from the land.

g. God's Display of Grace

The facet of grace was seen throughout the Dispensation of Law in two ways. First, the sacrificial system was provided because the Jews were not able to keep all 613 commandments. Whenever the individual Jew failed, this could be covered by the sacrificial system as a means for restoring the sinner. The sacrificial system would not take away the sin, neither was any Jew ever saved merely because he brought a sacrifice to the Tabernacle or the Temple. As in every age, the Jew was saved by grace through faith. His faith was the element that saved him, but his faith had to have content. In this case, the content of his faith was the sacrificial system. When he brought that sacrifice to the Tabernacle or Temple, he had the faith that his sins would be covered and fellowship would be restored by the means of the shedding of blood.

The second way grace was displayed during this dispensation was by God's provision of judges, kings, prophets, and the promised Messiah. Judges were given to deliver the Jews from subjugation to various peoples. Righteous kings were provided to give them a kingdom of righteousness and justice. Prophets were sent in order to expound the law, to call the people back to obedience, to remind them of where they had failed, and to call them to repentance. The Messiah came to provide salvation to all who accept Him.

6. The Dispensation of Grace: Acts 2:1 to Revelation 19:21

a. The Name

While grace was evident in all other dispensations, it is in this dispensation that a very unique display of grace was manifested that was different from all former displays of grace. Concerning this dispensation, John 1:17 states: *For the law was given through Moses; grace and truth came through Yeshua Messiah.* This verse does not mean that there was no law before Moses. But before Moses, the laws were rather minimal. Suddenly, with Moses, there is a unique display of laws—613 of them, in fact.

Certainly, God was gracious before the coming of *Yeshua*, for there are many evidences of God's grace throughout the pages of the Old Testament. However, with the coming of the Messiah, there was a totally unique display of grace that was not experienced heretofore. So the Dispensation of Law does not mean there was no law before that time any more than the Dispensation of Grace means there was no grace before this time. It means there was a unique display of it.

This dispensation extends from Acts 2:1, with the beginning of the indwelling ministry of the Holy Spirit at Pentecost, through Revelation 19:21. It covers the entire period of the Church Age and also includes the seven years of the Great Tribulation.

b. The Chief Person

The key person was the Apostle Paul, who received the revelation concerning the Dispensation of Grace. It was no accident that he received more revelation than any other apostle. Most of the letters or epistles of the New Testament were written by him. And so it is no surprise that it was he that received that special revelation concerning *the dispensation of that grace of God* in Ephesians 3:2. He, more than any other apostle, is the key person for this dispensation.

c. Man's Responsibility

Man's responsibility is obedience to the New Covenant, which means to accept the gift of righteousness that God offers to all men through *Yeshua* the Messiah. The point of Romans 5:15-18 is that man is responsible to accept *the gift of righteousness* that God offers to all men through the Messiah of Israel.

d. Man's Specific Test

The specific test is simply this: Will man accept the free gift of salvation on God's condition? God's condition is that it can only be received through the Messiah. Will humanity, as a whole, accept God's offer of the free gift of salvation by the simple act of faith in the Messiahship of *Yeshua*?

e. Man's Failure

As with all previous dispensations, the present one will also end in failure. This can be seen in two ways: first, most men will reject the gift. The majority of humanity will not come to a saving knowledge of *Yeshua* the Messiah. This is true for the past, the present, and certainly also for the future.

The second way failure is going to be seen is that the very organism that has knowledge of the truth, the church, will become apostate and will even turn away from that truth. It is already a shame that men in general reject the truth, but when the church itself rejects the truth from which it was called, that is sadder still.

f. Man's Judgment

This age, the Age of Grace, will also end with the facet of judgment: the Great Tribulation. The Great Tribulation will fall upon the whole world in general, because humanity in general has failed to accept the free gift of salvation offered through *Yeshua* the Messiah. Also the unbelieving, visible church will go into the Tribulation and suffer the wrath of God. But the believing, invisible Church, the true believers in the church, will be taken out of this earth before the Tribulation ever starts.

g. God's Display of Grace

It is in this area that we also see the facet of grace. Grace will be seen through the Rapture of the Church in that the invisible Church—the true Body of the Messiah, composed of all true believers—will be raptured out of this earth. Even those who have died, their bodies will be resurrected, so that even their bodies will not be on this earth during the seven years of the Great Tribulation. The Rapture will be a unique display of grace in the Dispensation of Grace.

Even during the Tribulation, there is the salvation of "an innumerable number of Gentiles." Throughout the Tribulation, individual Jews will come to believe, including 144,000 men. At the end of the Tribulation, the whole nation will come to saving faith. That, too, will show grace.

7. The Dispensation of the Kingdom or Millennium: Revelation 20:1-10

a. The Names

The seventh and last dispensation also has two names: the Dispensation of the Kingdom or the Dispensation of the Millennium. The first name emphasizes the Messiah's rule over this particular planet. The second name emphasizes the length of this dispensation: one thousand years.

b. The Chief Person

The key person in this case will be the Messiah, because the Messiah Himself will be dispensing direct, new revelation upon which the new dispensation will be based (Is. 2:2-4).

c. Man's Responsibility

Man's responsibility will be obedience to the King and the new laws He will issue during this period. These new laws are simply called "Kingdom Law." In the Dispensation of the Kingdom, there will be "something old and something new." The old is the responsibility to respond to the demands of the New Covenant, which means to exercise faith in *Yeshua* the Messiah and His substitutionary death, burial, and resurrection. The new responsibility is obedience to the King, who will then be visible here on earth, and obedience to the laws He will issue.

d. Man's Specific Test

The test will be to accept the King as one's personal Savior. Everyone born during the Kingdom Age will still have to believe that *Yeshua* died for his sins, was buried, and rose again.

e. Man's Failure

There will also be the facet of failure in that future dispensation. Men will fail to accept the Messiah, and at the end of the Millennium, Satan will be able to deceive humanity once again. Man will encounter the best living conditions since the fall—a perfect government, a perfect environment, no hunger, no plagues, no illness, no sickness. Nevertheless, mankind will come together for one last revolt against God's authority by attempting to invade Israel and invade the Holy City itself.

f. Man's Judgment

The judgment in this dispensation will be the destruction of all these invading armies by fire out of Heaven.

g. God's Display of Grace

Grace will also be displayed during this particular dispensation in three major ways. First, during the Kingdom, there will be the fulfillment of all covenantal promises to Israel.

Second, all prophesies that have remained unfulfilled until this time will find their fulfillment during the Messianic Kingdom.

Third, it will be a period of prosperity for all mankind, a righteous government, a perfect environment, no plagues, no hunger, and no sickness. Those who come to faith in this period will receive immortality. At some point, the body moves from mortality to immortality, but believers in the Kingdom will not die. However, unbelievers will die at the age of one hundred (Is. 65:20).

When this seventh dispensation ends, history will move from the aspect of time to the aspect of eternity as it enters into the eternal state (Rev. 21:1-22:5).

8. Conclusion

In a very quick survey then, this is the general outline of the dispensations. There is a lot more detail that could be discussed, but that belongs to a separate study of the dispensations and dispensationalism. Here, we are concerned, of course, with a brief survey of the subject.[47]

---

[47] Suggestion 3 on page 142

C. Questions and Study Suggestions

Suggestion 1: It may assist you to journal through this part of the study the concepts brought to you that give insight to the very large view of how God manages His will through each period of time. Many truths will come to the forefront. They will open doors to your understanding of the character of God and His plan for mankind. Journal these insights and watch how the Holy Spirit draws your heart and mind into a close relationship with the sovereign God of the universe.

Question 1: What is the definition of a dispensation? What is each dispensation based on?

Suggestion 2: It may become immediately obvious to the student in the coming sections that these seven specific facets of the dispensation can be charted together. It becomes obvious that there is a defined plan through time. To see this as clearly as possible is also to understand it as clearly as possible. On the next page, you will find a template for this chart.

Prior to going through this chapter of study, write down what areas of Scripture you are most familiar with. As you discover insights, note them. Do you see God's Word in its context as you work through this understanding of the seven dispensations? Journal this discovery along with the task of creating the chart of the seven dispensations.

Suggestion 3: Take the online test for this section of the study of the Word of God found on http://ariel.org/come-and-see.htm under "The Dispensations of God (041)" quiz.

THE SEVEN DISPENSATIONS OF GOD							
A	B	C	D	E	F	G	H
1							
2							
3							
4							
5							
6							
7							

A: Dispensation and Scripture

B: Name(s)

C: Chief Person

D: Responsibility to Man

E: Specific Test

F: Specific Failure

G: Judgment

H: Divine Grace

Notes: This is merely a template. It may be that several columns fit on one page of notes while the rest of the columns flow to subsequent pages. Printed off, they may be taped together. The goal of this view is to see how God unfolds the dispensations through time.

CPSIA information can be obtained at www.ICGtesting.com
Printed in the USA
LVOW04s2340160115

423189LV00009B/57/P